Until the Last Pickle

A MEMOIR IN 18 RECIPES

YULIYA PATSAY

Copyright © 2023 by Yuliya Patsay

Illustrations © 2023 Lucy Giller, Author photo: Kim Thompson Steel

All rights reserved. No part of this publication may be reproduced, distributed, or transmitted in any form or by any means, including photocopying, recording, or other electronic or mechanical methods, without the prior written permission of the publisher, except in the case of brief quotations embodied in critical reviews and certain other non-commercial uses permitted by copyright law.

For permission requests, write to the author at:
yuliya@yuliyapatsay.com

Until the Last Pickle / Yuliya Patsay—1st ed.

ISBN Paperback: 978-1-956989-28-1
ISBN Hardcover: 978-1-956989-29-8

DEDICATION

This book is dedicated to families everywhere—however they choose to be defined;

To my мишпуха* [mishpuha], past, present, and future.

But especially to my roots—my mom Marina and my dad Peter, and to my little branches—my daughters.

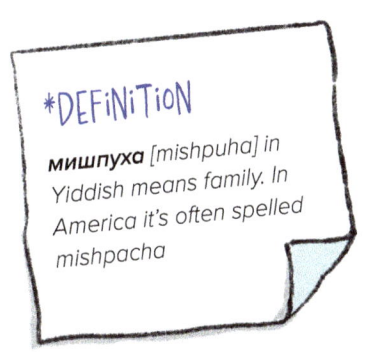

> ***DEFINITION**
>
> **мишпуха** [mishpuha] in Yiddish means family. In America it's often spelled mishpacha

PS Yes I know I left out my husband.
But who is he supposed to be in this analogy? My trunk? The soil?
The wind beneath my leaves? Ugh I give up!

WHO THIS BOOK IS FOR

This book is about identity, belonging, and bias. It's a collection of stories, photos, recipes, and anecdotes that show what life was like for us in the former Soviet Union and as new immigrants, and about how we incorporate our multiple (frequently competing) identities today.

In a weird way, I wrote this book for everyone I have ever met.

And everyone who I will meet.

Please to enjoy.*

But specifically, it's for you if...

- You've recently discovered that you're 23% Eastern European and you're yearning for something more profound than Hollywood's portrayal of us (as evil army general, corrupt business owner, pushy big busted broad) to illuminate the customs of this part of the world? Da? Buy this book. What are you waiting for? (Oops, I guess I am a walking cliche...)
- You like learning about cultures and food? And more specifically, perhaps you've always been curious about the diverse cuisine (encompassing myriad countries....in a way that definitely borders on cultural appropriation...) which includes such exotic dishes as herring under a fur coat and meat jello? Mmmmm...meat jello (not as gross as it sounds, I promise.)
- You're feeling nostalgic about your Soviet-era childhood and want to reminisce about the cultural phenomenons and foodstuffs from this special time? Then come walk down memory lane with me. If I'm misremembering it all

PROVERB ALERT
before the start of any meal we all wish each other **приятного аппетита** *[priyatnovo appetita] or Bon appetit*

- ~~(come on, that's poetic license, people!)~~, at the very least, you'll have something to argue with me about.
- You are traveling (via time machine) to the former Soviet Union and need some advice? I've got that! I provide a list of cultural landmines to avoid to guide you on your time-traveling journey to a land that no longer exists... maybe with good reason...
- Perhaps you are in a new relationship with someone who insists on putting mayonnaise and dill on everything and are looking for some support? Not only can I provide support, but I can provide recipes for you to share together, and if that fails, some mild hypnosis:...dill is delicious, dill is nutritious, dill is.... I'm sorry, is he putting dill on a dessert right now? Some people are beyond help.
- You have always wanted to party as hard as we former Soviet Union folk do? Hint: we're serving more than vodka at parties. (see the Special Occasions Food Ideas Spread)
- You enjoy an almost voyeuristic level of insight into the lives of celebrities? You're in luck. This is basically a tell-all. What's that now? I'm NOT a celebrity, and no one cares how I like my bread buttered? Shut up! The book is already in the cart.... submit order... submit order...

CALLOUTS

Throughout the book, you'll see different types of callout bubbles:

Definition:

definitions of Russian or Yiddish words used

Proverb alert:

peppered throughout the book are relevant Soviet Sayings* or as we call them "пословица" poslovitsa or "поговорка" pogovorka.

Now & then:

an opportunity to compare and contrast life in the Soviet Union and life in the United States

Fun fact:

or not a fun fact, your call

> ***DEFINITION**
>
> While in English, both of those words translate to "proverb," there is, in fact, a distinction between these two concepts. A пословица (poslovitsa) typically has a moral contained therein, while a pogovorka (поговорка) is more of a common saying. These vary by region.

TABLE OF CONTENTS

> **PROVERB ALERT**
>
> *Аппети́т прихо́дит во вре́мя еды́ | Appetite comes with eating. when you see a table laden with goodies you will get an appetite even if you didn't have one before (works for everything in life, the idea is just get started on whatever you're starting on...like reading this book for instance)*

INTRODUCTION
Before We Begin, A Few Disclaimers 5
Cast Of Characters My Family 7
FAQs 9
    Фаршмак *Farshmak* 11
What Is Distinctly Soviet? 14
    Малосольные огурцы *Half Sour Pickles* 20
    Соленые помидоры *Pickled Tomatoes* 21
Distinctly Soviet Food Equations 23

SPECIAL OCCASIONS
Procurement For The Proletariat 31
Special Occasions Mix and Match Chart 34
Marina's Salad Masterpieces 38
    Салат Оливье *Salat Olivie* 39
    Винегрет *Vinaigrette* 40
    Шуба *Herring Under Fur Coat* 41
What You Can Make With Mayo & Eggs 42

Новый Год [Novoi god] New Year's 43
Your Soviet New Year's Eve Checklist 48
    Холодец *Babushka Liliya's Holodetz (aka Aspic)* . . 53
    Babushka Liliya's Блинчики *Blinchiki (crepes)* . . . 54

Свадьба [Svadba] Wedding 55
Memories, Mementos & Menus 60
But First? First, There Was "Us." 62
If You Want To Marry Your Cousin, Don't Come To Reno, Nv. . . 65
Wedding Traditions: Yours, Mine, And Ours 67

День рождения [Den rozhdeniya] Birthday 73
The Five Best Birthday Cakes Countdown 77
    Мечта *My Mother in Law's Mechta* 78
    Вафельный торт *Waffle Cake* 80
Birthdays: There, Then, Now 81

Three Cultures For The Price Of One 85
   Holiday Calendar 88
   A Very Un American Thanksgiving, My Favorite Holiday 91
      Gefilte Fish 93
      Солёная рыба Salted Salmon 95
   Religion And Theology In The USSR 96
   Holy Water 97
   My Emerging Jewish Identity, A Timeline 99
   I Was Brought To This Country To Make My Mother Cry 103

EVERYDAY CELEBRATIONS
FAQ Part Two 111
      Yelena's Sneaky Сырники Sirniki 114
Mini Bites From The Garden 117
Tears Of My Tree 119
The Food In/Out List 121
      Борщ Borscht 122
      Капустняк или Щи Kapustnyak or Schii 124
      Голубцы Golubsti 125
      Пирожки Pirozhki 127
      (Can't Live Without My) Котлеты Kotleti 130
The Lure Of Sweet Sweet Birch Tree Sap (Березовый Сок) 131
Flavors I'll Never Forget 132
Tetya Polya's Farm 133
Quiz 135
Goodbye America, Longing To Leave 136
Breakfast Buffet 138
A Comedy Of Errors 141
Lost In Translation 142
Coveting (Fluorescent Curly Cues Of Perfection) 143
I Didn't Become A Supermodel, But I Did Get To Try A Root Beer Float ... 146
The One Where My Mom Bakes Cakes 148
Story Snacks: Kippers, Fettuccine Alfredo, Ketchup And Kix 150
How To Be A Good Host/Guest 153
Conclusion/Epilogue 155
Acknowledgments 157
References 158
Glossary 160
Proverbs/Sayings In Order Of Appearance 165
Author Bio 169
Book Blurbs 170

INTRODUCTION

If someone has just finished fumbling through pronouncing my name (it's Yuliya*, like Goo-lia) the next question is inevitable: so, where are you from?

I never know how to answer this. I'm from the Soviet Union, a place that exists only in the past. I was born in the town of Хмельницкий (Khmelnytskyi) which is now Western Ukraine, and immigrated to San Francisco when I was just about eight years old.

From the moment that plane touched down, I began living in different worlds: speaking a language, living by a set of values, and adopting a particular way of being in the (American) world while embodying a fairly different persona at home. It's not exactly that I have one foot in two countries, it's more like three toes in the old world and the rest of me here, but with my soul forever divided.

Thirty years later, I still straddle two or more different cultures—that of my home country and my family of origin, and that of my adopted country and the family I am building. Mix in some confusion over my religion (my mom's family is Jewish, and my dad's had me baptized into Russian Orthodoxy in secret, so.... yeah...#awkward), and I'm left feeling like I'm always adapting to fit in and never quite belonging.

I guess you can see how an innocent question like "where are you from" can leave me reeling. Because at the core of that question is the bigger question, *who*

> *NOW & THEN
>
> *The formal pronunciation of my name "Yuliya" is only something I started going by in college. Prior to that I went by 'Juila' to seem more American. And prior to that everyone in the Soviet Union called my by the short version of my name [Yul'a]*

are you, and how do you fit into this world?

Many of my disagreements with my parents center around this core conflict. They often ask me, dismayed, *"Who raised you?"* when I fail to live within the code of ethics that they are so certain they have handed down to me. The thing is, I never went through a rebellious teenage phase, and only now, in my late thirties, have I begun to truly forge my own path. I've been carefully examining the set of values they live by, picking each one up and holding them up to judge: does this truly make sense for me?

One particular point of contention with my parents was how often we should spend time together as an (extended) family. We have a small-ish extended family, but our tradition has been to celebrate every single birthday, wedding anniversary, every major American holiday as well as every major Jewish holiday, and even some distinctly Soviet holidays…which altogether added up to ~~what any reasonable person would feel~~ what I felt was an unreasonable amount of time to spend together. For example, from mid-March to mid-April, we have four birthdays and one wedding anniversary, which meant we would see each other at least weekly, if not more!

This was madness, in my opinion.

I kept proposing that we think about a monthly celebration or shifting away from celebrating every birthday and just concentrating on the milestone birthdays. My plan didn't get full family approval, and I went grumbling along from celebration to celebration, lamenting my lack of willpower to avoid birthday cake!

Eventually, I realized that, for my parents and extended family, putting on these celebrations and cooking these particular dishes was a way of passing down culture. And since I was already spending a disproportionate amount of time eating and celebrating, I decided to make the best of it. I began a modest project to document **what** we celebrate and **how** we celebrate. I had planned to collect the recipes we have in our family and perhaps even create a recipe book for my children to enjoy, all while spending some quality time with my relatives (and eating some great food.)

Then the pandemic happened. [Whomp. Whomp.]

And I spent three months confined to my home with my husband and children. (San Francisco = *hella*-strict COVID policies.)

And as we postponed my Aunt's 50th birthday celebration, blew out birthday candles by Duo, spent Passover on Zoom (the Dayenus really seem to go on forever thanks to the sound lag), and on and on, I began to understand just what a gift it is to get together in person and break bread (or matzoh) together.

The pandemic created an even more important question to attempt to answer for my modest recipe project, **why** do we celebrate?

That's how this book was born.

Three generations from now, my **descendants**[1] might say, "Oh, I think my grandparents came from over there," but I want more than that! I want to provide a touchstone for the traditions and the culture that we pass on. The food we prepare, the songs we sing around a campfire, the literature and movies we revere—they all provide the foundation for who we are and what we value. I want my kids (and their kids and theirs) to understand why these celebrations were so important, why we fought for these traditions, why we broke the law to practice our customs, and why who we are matters.

In this book, I'll be sharing personal stories and a handful of recipes and how-to's. Feel free to eat with your eyes, nibble on favorites, or devour every word.

---

[1] Note the subtle indoctrination of my children with the assumption that they procreate. What can I say, I learned from the best.

It's my book, and I'll write a second introduction if I want to...

As I began to work on this book, the conflict in Eastern Ukraine escalated and led to the Russian invasion. Typing these words feels ludicrous like I'm living in some kind of alternate reality. While the political machinations behind these events may be complex and the narrative nuanced, the outcome is clear: millions of displaced people—many women and children, the landscape warped, and lives forever lost or changed.

When battle lines between cousins are drawn, and blood is spilled, what remains?

Even though my personal journey out of the former Soviet Union was much less dramatic and dire than the current exodus, what remained for me was the memories of a place and time, the tastes of childhood, the smells around a kitchen table, and the faces gathered around it for a toast.

None of this (gestures to book in front of you) seemed worthwhile to explore while this conflict raged (and continues to rage), and I wasn't able to pick up this project for months. After all, what would be the point of a lighthearted, humorous memoir about a Soviet-era childhood when the region is in chaos, and people are in pain?

Perhaps there is no "point."

But now more than ever, I feel compelled to capture a piece of the world from my memories, a place that now exists only in our hearts.

BEFORE WE BEGIN, A FEW DISCLAIMERS...

1. On the use of the words Soviet or Soviet-inspired. What I mean by this is the period of 1922–1991, or more specifically, the time frame of my immediate family's experience—roughly the 1940s to the early 90s. It should not be construed as an endorsement of socialism or communism or any of the other terrible isms that the word may conjure. It is simply that, in the place I was born, at the time I was born, the culture I experienced was not Ukrainian and not Russian (and certainly not Jewish!) but something entirely separate—it was Soviet—and that word will have to do.

2. On the use of the memories of an unreliable narrator. I was seven years old when I left the former Soviet Union, so the recollections contained in this memoir, particularly about that time period are murky at best.

3. On the objects in the camera viewfinder (they may appear more perfect than they are.) This is a filtered version of our life. Much in the way that you would plate a dish to be served, this plated version of who we are and how we celebrate is also curated. Please keep in mind this is definitely less of a

"how-to" book and more of a "how-we-do-it" book—just one family's neurotic set of rules for doing things. Ditto for the recipes. (My mom in particular would like you all to know that she is not personally responsible for the accuracy of any of these recipes.) And speaking of families, this book is a love letter to my family, but as anyone who's had a family knows it is not always pretty, sometimes there's too much vodka, and the whole thing ends in tears (no? Just us?) But the love is fierce and the food is damn good. So use common sense, don't mix beer and vodka* (unless you're on a budget), and don't drink and drive. Enjoy!

> ***PROVERB ALERT**
>
> **всё перемелица, мука будет** - everything will be ground together and you will have flour. This expression is used to say that no matter the conflicts that happen it will be ok because we are family and we love each other. A similar American saying is "everything comes out in the wash."

> ***PROVERB ALERT**
>
> **Водка без пива деньги на ветер** [vodka bez piva dengi na veter] vodka without beer is money wasted. Basically to get your bang for the buck, drink both together.

CAST OF CHARACTERS
MY FAMILY

1. **Author** - Your average neurotic, not always nice Jewish girl (who's also Soviet *and* Ukrainian *and* American!)
2. **Husband** - Your average android-like husband: needs maintenance and downtime, speaks rarely, but when he does, he is quite witty and wise.
3. **Mom** - How do I see her? Oh, that's easy to answer! She's beautiful! Radiant! So smart! Pretty bossy sometimes. She wants everything to be just so.
4. **Dad** - He looks like a member of the mob, but he's a teddy bear! Well, a teddy bear who drives a cab and can curse like a sailor (in six languages.)
5. **Mother-in-Law** - A gem of a human being. No seriously, I lucked out. I just wish my birthday was three times a year so she could make her famous cake for me.
6. **Father-in-Law** - Thoughtful toast giver and chess teaching wizard.
7. **Aunt** - She had to wash my cloth diapers when she was twelve years old; it's possible she still holds a grudge. She can make an authentic tiramisu, and is generally always whipping something tasty up in the kitchen.
8. **Uncle** - The man crazy enough to marry into this mishigana mishpacha, surely there's something wrong with him…
9. **My cousins** - the first of our family born in America! And as a bonus? Really cool people!
10. **Maternal Grandparents** - Babushka Lilya - the child whisperer and Deda Vova - the poet. They've hosted me for many a sleepover and fed me ice cream in bed (grandparents RULE!)

Author's parents Dad Peter and Mom Marina

11. **Maternal Great Grandparents, parents of Deda Vova** – Abram, the Jew (and the actor), and Musya, the Ukrainian (whose job it was to round me up for dinner throughout my Soviet childhood.)
12. **Maternal Grandpa's sister and family** – Tanya, Vova, Sasha, Serezha – a colorful cast of characters that shared our apartment (communal living for the win!)
13. **Maternal Great Grandparents, parents of Baba Liliya** – Maria (Manya) with the movie star looks and heart of gold and Mikhael who was always tinkering with something
14. **Paternal Grandparents – Baba Shura and Deda Aleksei** – I have just a handful of memories with them, but each memory is the epitome of childhood.
15. **My children** – Describing my children is impossible. They are perfect and infuriating at the same time, and I love them just the way they are.

And everyone else in my extended family with a special shout out to my family still in Ukraine! If I listed everyone it could take eleven more pages.

Author's Maternal Great Grandparents Abram and Musya with Mom Marina as a little girl

Author's Maternal Great Grandparents Maria and Mikhael with their children

FAQS

And now some answers to questions that I get asked* all of the time...

Q: Where are you from?
    A: I'm based in beautiful San Francisco. (And yes I like the fog.)

Q: But like where are you from "from"? You look ethnic...
    A: *looks around awkwardly* Thank you? I'm originally from the former Soviet Union. I'm from a country you've probably never heard of. I'm from Ukraine. You've probably heard of it.

Q: Oh, so then you must speak Ukrainian?
    A: No Dad, you know very well that when I was growing up the Soviet Union insisted that everyone speak Russian, so while I did learn Ukrainian as a second language, when I immigrated to the US I lost Ukrainian and gained English.*

Q: But Soviet and Russian are the same thing, right?
    A: Nyet.
    In some ways, Soviet is easier to define as it is limited to a particular time period (See next question). But defining "Russia" is trickier. "Russia" is really a shorthand for a series of different states with different names and different boundaries, depending on what period of its millennia-long history we are looking at.

> *NOW & THEN
> Optional drinking game for fellow former Soviet Union folks: take a shot for every question YOU have had to answer

> *FUN FACT
> And since I learned English by watching Star Trek the Next Generation with my dad, I might have also "gained" Klingon.

Q: So, what was the Soviet Union exactly?

A: Ah yes and now it's time for a super quick and painless history lesson on the former Soviet Union.

The Soviet Union (officially known as the Union of Soviet Socialist Republics) was a socialist state that spanned multiple republics from the time period of 1922–1991 during which it was the largest country in the world. Life in the Soviet Union varied dramatically during each change in leadership from Lenin to Stalin to Khrushchev, then Brezhnev, and *finally** Gorbachev. The Soviet Union "collapsed" in 1991.

> *FUN FACT
>
> Between Brezhnyev and Gorbachev there were two short-lived general secretaries - Chernenko and Andropov who both died in office.

Q: Do you just eat caviar every day?

A: Depends who's asking. Why, you interested? Because I got a guy, you need a guy? I'll hook you up.

And yes, while there is probably no other food that's more closely associated with Russia as caviar is, the reality is that this was a land of extremes – with everything from poverty at best and mass famine at worst to abundance and excess especially in the Tsarist era. Even during Communism, party elites had access to abundance while the rest stood in line for bread.

And now let me ask you a question, have you ever heard of Jewish caviar? I hadn't until my mom mentioned that some refer to the following herring recipe as Jewish caviar!

Фаршмак
Farshmak

Ingredients

¼ onion
1 pickled herring filet, *deboned and cleaned, if very salty rinse thoroughly*
¼ granny smith apple
2-3 hard boiled eggs
70-100g butter

Instructions

- Use food processor to combine herring and eggs.
- Grate apple and onion on a small grater, squeeze out juice and combine with herring and eggs.
- Melt butter, give it time to cool and then add to the mix.
- Refrigerate and serve.

Q: Forget caviar, aren't Ruskis just all about that vodka?

A: ~~Yes!~~ Well kind of, the beverages most likely to be in every peasant and baron's home were kvas, *braga**, mead, and beer. But by the time the Soviet Union came together, vodka was the most popular and most important drink.

> ***FUN FACT**
> Braga is fermented rye and is approximately 20 proof

Q: But my brother visited Russia years ago and he told me there's a vodka vending machine.

A: *He's probably thinking of a soda vending machine (газированная вода.)*

Picture a machine, roughly refrigerator size. On one side of the dispenser, you would get a glass, give it a perfunctory rinse, and then select either plain bubbly water (1 kopeck) or add flavored syrup (3 kopecks.)* The most popular flavored syrups were pear, citrus, cream soda, and tarkhun, which was similar to tarragon but with a sweeter flavor. You'd drink your "soda" and then return that glass and give it another perfunctory rinse so that the next person could GRAB THE EXACT SAME GLASS and take their turn. Efficiency and hygiene all in one!

> ***FUN FACT**
> As the machines were not terribly sophisticated, cheating frequently ensued. Some clever lads (and lasses) drilled a hole in their 3 kopeck piece, tied a string to it and fished it out to use again!

Q: Ok, so, what exactly is Russian or Soviet food?

A: *This is an excellent question. Before we get to the "what," let's address the "how."* Perhaps the most distinct aspect of eating like a Soviet (or eating like a Russian) is the order in which courses are served and the types of food served during each course. Unlike the words "soup course" or "entree" or dessert, the Russian words for [aspects of a meal] are первое [pervoye] first course, второе [vtoroye] second course, and третье [treteye] third course. As their name implies, first course, second course, and third course, the order of the meal is perhaps even more important than the content of the meal itself. In fact, the very first Russian cookbooks which were printed at the end of the 18th century gave equal attention to presenting an order of dishes as they did with any individual dish.

The short answer to what we ate is—anything and everything. A Soviet-era cook had to be most resourceful and inventive based on the availability of products and that varied wildly throughout the history of the Soviet Union. Popular foodstuffs associated with this place are potatoes, cabbage, wheat, and all products derived from it.

Q: Salo. Dear god, why?!!

A: This is another excellent question! And before we get to the "why" let us first answer "what"—what is salo*? Salo is (essentially) lard. And now back to why, this author is personally somewhat repulsed by it, but if beauty is in the eye of the beholder, the same is true that tasty is in the mouth of the eater. A friend supplies that "the salty, and a tiny bit crunchy piece of salo on a slice of Ukrainian bread just brings back good memories."

> *FUN FACT
>
> Assimilation meant that in some parts of the country certain foods or dishes were popular while in other parts people may have never even heard of them, salo is mostly a Ukrainian delicacy.

Q: Did you really have to wait in line for food?

A: No it was a carefully orchestrated publicity campaign to keep away bourgeois capitalists.

(Yes. And supermarkets weren't really a thing, so you would have to stand in multiple lines in multiple stores. Knowing that, just imagine how much sympathy I have for my kids when they complain to me about being bored...)

Q: Look, I can speak Russian—baBUshka!

A: That's not a question. Also you're saying it wrong it's BAbushka (emphasis on the first syLAble) And while we're at it it's pirozhKI, not piROshki.

Q: So what is Soviet style? You seem to say that a lot

A: Ah! This is an excellent question, let us begin...

WHAT IS DISTINCTLY SOVIET?

There are two ways to think about what is distinctly Soviet.

One is, what was the Soviet way while the Soviet Union existed?

And the other is, what is Soviet that is carried forward in all of us who left and even impacts the way we raise our children? So Soviet that some of us who were even born in America have a distinctly Soviet way about us?

(Of course the third, which is to look at the impact that the Soviet mentality has on the countries that remain today, I cannot speak to with any authority.)

Regardless of there or here, or then or now, to me the Soviet mentality, in a nutshell, is – admit nothing, deny everything, never sign your name on a document you don't understand that is legally binding that cannot be undone... unless... it's somehow going to benefit you, and always be ready to trick the authorities through a combination of smoke and mirrors and staging an elaborate theatrical performance on the spot.

But what else? Besides long lines, salo, and vodka there are some distinctly Soviet ways of being, customs let's say. Regardless of where we ended up in the world, these are the things that never left us:

Hospitality/Food is kind of a big deal/Keep the party going/Reciprocity

> ***FUN FACT**
> My mom and dad always turn on the lights and shout out сделай праздник "make it a holiday" when we sit down for a meal together.

- The most enduring legacy is хлебосольство [khlebosolstvo] or hospitality. Though we may disagree on just about everything else (politics, what constitutes a great film, how many layers of clothing a child needs to go outside in) without a doubt my parents and I are completely on the same page about what hospitality means: at a bare minimum it means food and drink for your guests, a comfortable chair to sit in, and bright

> *DEFINITION*
> хлеб и соль - [hleb i sol']
> bread and salt

lights for a festive atmosphere*. Basically if you haven't offered someone a beverage within the first ten minutes of them entering your dwelling, you may as well turn in your hostess badge. Anytime you have a guest, you greet them with хлеб и соль*. It's possible that this tradition evolved from necessity, since at the beginning of the 20th century, "peasants got almost two-thirds of their daily calories from grains.[2]" But regardless of the reason, this custom evolved to represent hospitality, the word for warm hospitality is literally bread хлеб + salt соль combined= хлебосольство.

- Speaking of hospitality, Soviet hospitality is next level. The expectation is that you give your guests the best of everything. There are several proverbs that highlight that the best is saved for guests.
    - ✦ отдать всё до последней рубахи [otdat' vse to posledniy rubahi] to give everything away until the last shirt! We'll get to the paradox of not having any food but being able to serve your guests food in a bit.
    - ✦ сначала накорми потом расспроси [snachala nakormi potom rasprosi] feed someone first, ask questions later.
    - ✦ Коль пошла такая пьянка режь последний огурец [kol' poshla takaya pyanka, rezh posledniy ogorez] if the party is still going then serve everything until the last pickle.
- Similarly, when you visit someone else's home you always bring something. It's customary to bring something - a homemade treat, flowers for women—easy enough, alcohol, candy—particularly tricky to do in Soviet times.

> *FUN FACT*
> Every Soviet parent will tell you to never visit someone empty handed. My mother in law is fond of saying *"я не могу прийти с пустыми руками"* I cannot go somewhere with my hands empty.

---

[2]   Alison K. Smith, Cabbage and Caviar: A History of Food in Russia (London: Reaktion, 2021), 34.

- Dropping in on friends, or neighbors was a big part of life in the Soviet Union. Not everyone had a phone so often you just made plans when you ran into someone on the street. We frequently invited people over or went to each other's houses known as ходить в гости [hodit v gosti] particularly if you happened to have procured something special that you could угостить [ugostit] your guests with.

> ***FUN FACT**
> *The Soviet animated version of Winnie the Pooh featured an entire episode dedicated to visiting your friends particularly in order to get a bite to eat.*

- In some ways our relationships with friends and acquaintances could be very transactional. I invite you to my house and I expect you to invite me next time. Especially because food is tough to come by so since I've made the effort and hosted you then I expect you to do the same. In some ways, this is still the way we do things, if you host someone it's quite customary to expect them to be the next ones to host, that way we spread the ~~burden~~ joy of hosting around fairly.

> ***FUN FACT**
> *The word for guest is* **гость** *[gost] and the word to provide hospitality to that guest or treat them is* угостить *[ugostit].*

Bargains

- Getting a bargain and telling everyone (or absolutely no one) how great a bargain it was. Do you have that one friend who bought a designer dress for $30 and tells everyone she knows it only cost $30 instead of letting them think that it broke the bank? Chances are her name is Vika and she's Soviet (or would get along famously with one.) Do you also have that one friend that will take how much something cost them to their grave? Also a high probability of Soviet roots (or just good common sense.)

Taking care of one's appearance/being purposeful with one's appearance and actions

- There are several popular children's stories that illustrate how important one's appearance and presence of mind is:
    - ✦ Мойдодыр [Moidodir] – a terrifying tale of a rogue bathroom sink that chases after a filthy child until he is scrubbed clean against his will which reforms him into a clean, outstanding student, at which point everything starts going his way
    - ✦ Федорино горе [Fedorina gorye] – a woeful story of an old lady who took poor care of her belongings and didn't clean them so they all got up and walked away until she repented, begged them to come back, and promised she'd never do it again
    - ✦ Рассеянный [Rasseyaniy]– a hilarious poem about a man who was so scatter-brained that he put his pants on as a shirt, wore a frying pan for a hat and missed his train to work
- Shoes off and тапочки "tapochki" (slippers)* on—you always take your shoes off at a Former Soviet person's house! Or else!
- You don't just have clothes. You have clothes with a designated purpose - house clothes, street clothes, school clothes and you NEVER sit on the bed in your street clothes.
- Neatness was of paramount importance—in school, we had uniforms that we were expected to keep clean and tidy, nails trimmed, hair combed or arranged in a hairstyle, and shoes polished.

> *FUN FACT*
> *In the Former Soviet Union (FSU) you would often bring a pair of shoes with you to work because the streets particularly in winter were dirty and wet.*

We are a superstitious bunch

- Warding off the evil eye was of particular concern. The term for the evil eye* is сглазить [zglazit] or literally to look at someone and create

> *FUN FACT*
> *These are not necessarily people who are evil themselves, they are just cursed with the evil eye and the terrible responsibility that comes with it.*

ill for them as a result. There are people that are known to have the evil eye and are capable of giving this look and there were two recommended remedies to combat this: булавка [bulavka] wearing a pin on your clothes or wearing a red thread.
- No handing things or hugging/kissing through a threshold.
- If you're returning after you've left the house for any reason you have to look in a mirror before you leave again.
- If a black cat crosses the street in front of you, it's bad luck. Similarly if someone crosses the street in front of you with empty buckets, also bad luck.

Food is a big deal to come by so for goodness sake, don't waste it!

- Общество чистых тарелок [obchestvo chistih tarelok] – the society of clean plates, means you never leave food on the plate, you must finish every last bite.
- Children were often coaxed into finishing food by being asked to take bites on behalf of other people за маму [za mamu] for Mom за папу [za papu] for Dad.

The masochistic Soviet Soul

- Тоска [toska]—a uniquely Russian word that means both longing, nostalgia, and suffering all in one.
- Our people have had to endure harsh climates, unstable political regimes, oppression, lack of resources, and on and on, therefore the legacy of suffering is as familiar as mother's milk. If we aren't suffering, are we even Soviet?

How shall I put this….Rudeness

(picture a Soviet-era customer service rep at any casual establishment saying…) Sit down. *Please to be welcome!*

This, which some might call this brusqueness and others rudeness, might stem from the idea that customer service simply didn't exist in the Soviet Union, it's a capitalistic concept, especially in the service industry that is dependent on tips.

In a world where people had to stand in four separate lines a week just to put dinner on the table, combined with the elaborate system of owing and granting favors (which you'll learn more about in Procurement for the Proletariat) who had time for niceties?

Put it this way, when we were getting married our Soviet caterer scoffed at all the ideas we had about what we might serve at our wedding. Her point of view more or less was, "that's not what you want, I'll tell you what you want!" And she's not alone, if you ever have the distinct pleasure of purchasing goods at a Russian deli you may encounter this specific style of customer service yourself. (Just remember tips are optional!)

How Shall I put this....Bribing

In the Soviet Union things simply didn't get done without a little palm greasing. Any professional you visited be it doctor or mechanic was encouraged to do their best work with a little gift on the side. More on this later...

Resourcefulness

Given the harsh environmental and political climate we are nothing if not a highly resourceful people. We never let little things like five months of winter without access to fruits and vegetables deter us! So we pickled things. Lots and lots of things. Here are some.

Малосольные огурцы
Half Sour Pickles

Ingredients

cucumber
2 tbsp salt per 1 L of water
1 bunch of dill *(ideally old, still has flowers)*
3-5 garlic cloves per 1L to taste

Instructions

- Mix 1L of water with 2 level Tbsp salt to create a marinate or "rassol"
- Put dill and garlic in the bottom of a large jar
- Add pickles vertically and tightly in a jar
- You could add more dill and garlic to the middle layer
- To make them ready faster cut off the ends so the water gets in faster, and use warm water rather than cold
- Cover until the top
- Close with a cheesecloth (no lid!) and leave in a sunny place
- After 1 day they are 'malosolniye', put them in the refrigerator
- You can also add anything you like to the jar: celery hearts, pepper

Соленые помидоры [Solyoniye pomidori]
Pickled Tomatoes

Ingredients

5 ½ lbs tomato (pro tip: these must be the same size and same ripeness level)

2 tbsp salt per 1 L of water, we will need about 3

1 tsp sugar per 1 L of water

3-4 bay leaves

handful of peppercorns

2 chili peppers

celery leaves (the heart of the celery)

handful of juniper berries

3-6 garlic cloves

1 bunch of dill

Instructions

- Place chili pepper, juniper, peppercorns, and bay leaf, salt and sugar, with water in a pot and bring to a boil to create a marinade. Let this cool.
- In a large jar place dill, garlic, and celery and then arrange the tomatoes, once you have filled about half the jar repeat the layering dill, garlic, celery and continue layering tomatoes.
- Pour the marinade on top, make sure all of the spices are in the jar, water doesn't have to fit but the spices do.
- Close with a cheesecloth and place in a semi sunny spot (morning sun isn't ideal but afternoon is good.)
- Leave for a week.
- In a week lift the cheesecloth, if there is mold remove it and leave for a few days.
- Remove the cheesecloth and close the jar with a lid.
- Leave in the refrigerator for two weeks.

We take greetings and goodbyes pretty seriously

Whenever we are greeting someone it is done with a firm handshake, a hug, a kiss, a look in someone's eyes, and a direct acknowledgment of them. The same for goodbyes. You must take a moment and look the person that is leaving in the eye and say a hearty goodbye to them. I'm not sure if this comes from the idea that you never know if you're going to see these people ever again (because KGB), but whatever the reason. I'm pretty appreciative of this custom.

classic Soviet photo: dad, me, mom

DISTINCTLY SOVIET FOOD EQUATIONS

INGREDIENTS

doktorskaya kolbasa, lard

Докторская колбаса [doktorskaya kolbasa] Doctor's kielbasa

Сало [salo] Lard

Докторская колбаса + сало = любительская колбаса
[luybitelskaya kolbasa] Favorite Kielbasa

Doctor's kielbasa + lard = Favorite kolbasa

Russian food pyramid

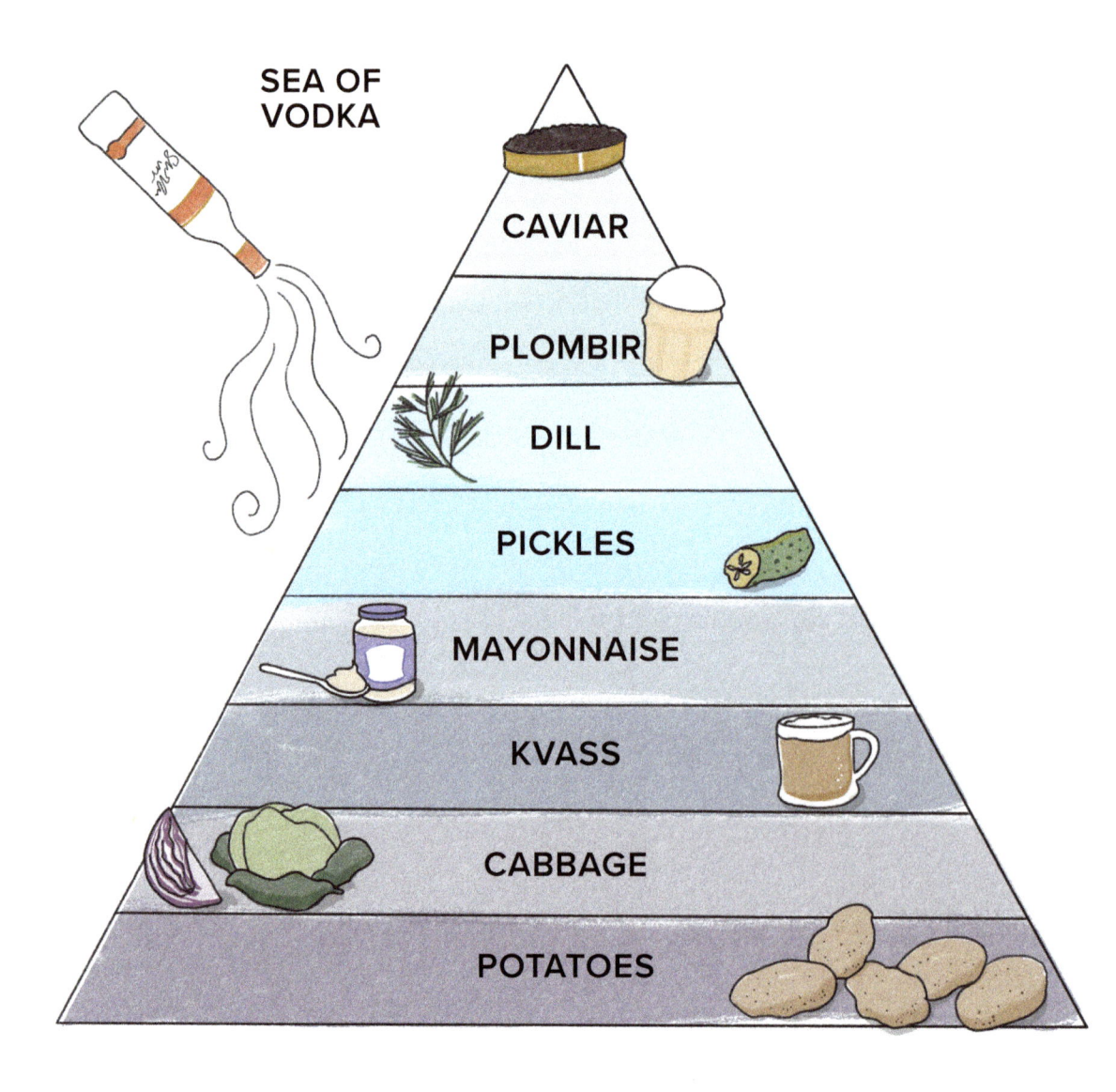

SEA OF VODKA

- CAVIAR
- PLOMBIR
- DILL
- PICKLES
- MAYONNAISE
- KVASS
- CABBAGE
- POTATOES

What's for dinner?

A dinner menu word problem for the middle class.

1st course:
вода с капустой
(voda s kapustoi)
water with cabbage
= water + cabbage

2nd course:
капуста без воды
kapusta bez vodi
cabbage without water
= cabbage − water

3rd course:
вода без капусты
voda bez kapusti
water without cabbage
= water − cabbage

A menu word problem for the other middle class.

1st course:
бульон с пельменями
bullion s pelminyami
broth and pelmeni
= broth + pelmeni

2nd course:
пельмени без бульона
pelmeni bez bullion
pelmeni without broth
= pelmeni − broth

3rd course:
бульон без пельменей
bullion bez pelmeney
broth without pelmeni
= broth − pelmeni

A menu word problem for the upper class

How dare you imply there is an upper class.
We are all equal in the eyes of the state.

SPECIAL OCCASIONS

The Soviet Union had a complicated relationship with holidays and special occasions. At one point the communist party experimented with eliminating weekends and holidays* altogether by implementing непрерывная рабочая неделя [nepreryvnaya rabochaya nedelya] a continuous production week, commonly referred to as непрерывка nepreryvka.

Between 1929–1931 as Joseph Stalin dragged the nation towards industrialization, the government shortened the seven-day week and created a five-day work week abolishing Saturdays and Sundays. Instead of weekends, they divided workers into five groups, assigned each a color (yellow, orange, red, purple, or green) and a coordinating day off.

The staggered schedule was known as непрерывка nepreryvka, or the "continuous workweek," since production never stopped. While the official aim might have been to increase production, the true aim was to destroy religion and social ties. Because this meant that husbands and wives might have different days off, making having a social life difficult and any organized religion practically impossible. By 1931 after much grumbling from the laborforce they went to a six-day week шестидневка [shestidnevka] where the sixth day was a holiday.

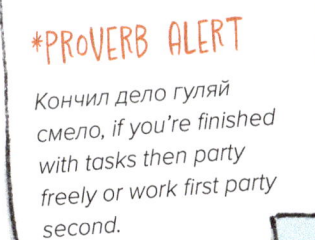

Theoretically this practice was abolished and society returned to a seven-day week by 1940. But practically speaking, even well into the 80s it was common to have a six-day work week, and a six-day school week. So take a guess how much

*PROVERB ALERT

Кончил дело гуляй смело, if you're finished with tasks then party freely or work first party second.

sympathy my parents have for me when I complain about my busy life?

What separates a special occasion from the everyday? In the Soviet Union holidays were referred to as красный день календаря "krasniy den kalendarya" or red calendar days. Quite literally these were days that were printed in red ink on the calendar. There were red calendar days on official state-sponsored holidays. But plenty of other special occasions did not warrant corresponding red ink on the calendar.

All religious events certainly were sacred but public celebrations of them were more than frowned upon in the communist state, it was simply against the law. That didn't stop people from finding creative ways to keep their religious and cultural traditions and practice them under the guise of a state-sanctioned event.

For example, the Russian Orthodox tradition of гробки [grobki] graves—which was typically celebrated the week after Easter (Пасха Pascha) was a practice where you would visit the graves of your ancestors, tidy the graves, and bring them Пасха pascha* and colored eggs. People went on observing this tradition by timing it to coincide with the state-sanctioned holiday of May 1st—International Workers Day. The name маевка mayovka was made by extending the word May.

> ***DEFINITION**
>
> *The word Пасха pascha means both Easter and the dome shaped culinary creations made especially for this holiday.*

PROCUREMENT FOR THE PROLETARIAT

The paradox* of the Soviet Union was that people celebrated and welcomed guests with a full table, regardless of the fact that hardly anything was available in stores.

How was central planning for food supposed to work in a socialist state? In theory, the central planning offices decided what crops to grow and how much to supply the population with all of the necessities of life.

However, central planning is something that has worked (thus far) only in theory and not in practice.

There are many reasons for this. Industries were heavily subsidized by the government, for starters. Food production was also subject to the whims of Soviet leaders like Kruschev's attempt to grow corn or Gorbachev's сухой закон[suhoi zakon] - dry laws.

But the principal reason for central planning failure is that at every step of the process, someone is skimming off the top (and more often than not, several someones). Therefore true supply and demand is never confirmed.

Every family skimmed off the top in their own way, or said another way—every family procured things differently. If anyone in your family worked in food production, or even in any food-related field like food testing, then they simply stole the supplies they had access to and bartered for the rest of what they needed. But regardless of where you worked, you could find something to barter with. My grandmother, for example, was a telephone switchboard operator and she bartered her ability to easily connect you.

Families also figured out their own effective tips and tricks for the barter economy. Like sending different family members to different stores simultaneously* or

> *PROVERB ALERT
>
> *Из гавна конфетку* - literally to make candy out of shit, when you have subpar ingredients and yet you can still turn them into something delicious. (technically speaking the word for shit in Russian is **дерьмо** [der'mo] and this is a hybrid Ukrainian Russian phrase as some in my family inevitably are

> *FUN FACT
>
> As soon as I could cross the street by myself, at five years old, my contribution to the procurement effort was standing in line for bread.

31

being first in line at a store, which meant you can buy whatever is available, hoard those supplies and then use them to barter later.

A handy glossary of terms related to the low key criminal activity of every Soviet Citizen

- Дефицит | **defitzit** | deficit* – products that are low supply, difficult to obtain*. Often scarcity was created artificially in order to increase the product's value and keep the barter system alive and well (related: delicacies which is a specialty food item like caviar.)

- Блат | **blaat** | favors – the system of using your connections* to garner favors (big favors), bartering for products or services, for example bringing your doctor something deficit (most often alcohol) in order to improve the treatment your doctor gives you or your family member.

- По блату | **Po Blatu** | through favors* – the answer to the question 'how did you obtain this?' through favors or 'po blatu.'

- Достать | **Do-stat** | To acquire – you know someone/have a connection that can somewhere through a series of favors locate something for you.

- Купить | **Kupit** | Buy – something you can actually buy in stores (after standing in several lines.)

- Найти | **Nayti** | To Find – going to several of the same kind of store (bread store for example) in order to obtain a specific product.*

PROVERB ALERT

Была бы курочка сварит и дурочка - if there was a chicken any idiot could cook it

PROVERB ALERT

Евреи не жалейте мяса в котлеты - Jews, don't spare meat for the cutlets, if you want something to taste good you have to use the correct ingredients (or any amount of the actual ingredient needed)

PROVERB ALERT

Не имей сто рублей, а имей сто друзей, It is better to have a hundred friends than a hundred rubles

PROVERB ALERT

Давать на лапу, to give onto the paw, to bribe someone

- Выбросили | **Viebrosiliye| Thrown away** – slang for something is finally being sold in stores.

- Дают |**Dayut| Giving|** – another slang term for what is sold in a particular store.

- Н.З. | **en ze| NZ|** an abbreviation for неприкосновенный запас [ne prekosnoveney zapas] your untouchable supply. This is food stuffs that you don't rely on every day, such as those in your pantry for example, where you store all of your non-perishables. Think of this as emergency supplies (in case of a party emergency), usually products that were deficit.

> ***NOW & THEN**
>
> *the practice of 'finding' carries over to this very day because even though the product offered in various Russian delis might be the same (herring, canned fish, etc) the distributors of these products are different. For example, in San Franciso, smoked herring is best procured from Europa Plus because they get it from a distributor in LA, whereas their competitor, a store just five blocks away -New World Market gets it from a NY distributor and (apparently) they are totally different!*

The argument FOR Soviet Style procurement

Famous Soviet Satirist, Arkady Raikin's has a popular skit about procurement.

In it he is shown as a passenger on a plane, enjoying a hearty meal full of 'deficit' products and making a case for the Soviet way of doing things. He explains that we work hard to obtain certain products, and our ability to do so effectively is met with a corresponding level of respect. He goes on to question whether we even want to live in a society where everything is available*, because if everyone can just get everything they need at any time then there is no one at the top of the respect pyramid so that "the director in charge of food distribution is walking around without any respect like a regular engineer!" If everything is special, then nothing is special.

> ***PROVERB ALERT**
>
> *Без труда не вытянешь рыбку из пруда | without work you will not pull the fish out of the hole |if you don't work hard you won't accomplish anything*

SPECIAL OCCASIONS
MIX AND MATCH/CHART

ASSORTED MEAT PLATE

- ☐ **Колбаса** [kolbasa] sausage
- ☐ **Бужанина** [buzhanina]
- ☐ **Ветчинна** [vetchinna] ham
- ☐ **Паштет** [pashtet] pate

ASSORTED FISH PLATE:

- ☐ Herring- pickled, smoked
- ☐ salmon,
- ☐ white fish
- ☐ Marinated fish

ЗАЛИВНЫЕ [ZALIVNIYE] JELLIED DISHES

- ☐ **Холодец** [holodets] aspic
- ☐ **Язик** [yazik] beef tongue
- ☐ **Заливное из осетрины** [zalivnoye iz osetriny] jellied/aspic sturgeon
- ☐ Gefilte fish

SANDWICHES БУТЕРБРОДИ [BUTERBRODI]

- ☐ Baked Bread with kippers
- ☐ baked baguette with tomato and cheese
- ☐ Bread with caviar, red or black

MARINATED & PICKLED THINGS

- ☐ Pickles
- ☐ Tomatoes
- ☐ Cabbage
- ☐ Watermelon
- ☐ Garlic
- ☐ Eggplant
- ☐ Peppers
- ☐ Mushroom

A NOTE ON CONDIMENTS, THEY ARE CRUCIAL

- ☐ Hot mustard
- ☐ **Хрен** [hren] horseradish
- ☐ Mayo & garlic

COMPOSED SALADS

- **Русский салат** [ruski salat] cucumber, tomato, onion
- **Оливье** [olivie] potato salad
- **Винегрет** [vinaigrette]
- **Салат под шубой** [shuboi] herring under fur coat
- **Грипозный** [gripozni]
- **Крабовый салат** [krabovyy salat] crab salad
- **Салат из печений трески** [salat iz pecheniy treski] cod liver salad

HOT APPETIZERS*

- **Блинчики** [blinchiki] crepes
- **Хачапури** [hachapuri] Georgian cheese bread
- **Грибной жюльен** [gribnoy zhyul'yen] cheesy mushroom
- Potatoes (mashed, boiled or fried), serve with or without dill
- **Пирожки** [pirozhki] buns with filling
- **Пельмени** [pelmeni] dumplings
- **Вареники** [vareniki*] dumplings
- **Налисники** [nalisniki] stuffed crepes
- **Чебуреки** [chebureki] deep fried turnovers

*FUN FACT

Hot appetizers in Russian are called 'promezhutki', or in translation they are things that are in between. They function as transitions between events, for example at a wedding if there has been a dance break for a while and you'd like to call people back to the table to resume the wedding program you serve a hot appetizer.

*FUN FACT

in Ukraine these are called vareniki and in Russia pierogi

HOT ENTREE**

- [ ] Roasted duck or goose
- [ ] Rabbit stew
- [ ] **Люля кебаб** [lyulya kebab] minced meat kebab
- [ ] **Шашлык** [shashlik] grilled cubes of meat
- [ ] **Циплята табака** [tzipliyata tabaka] pan fried chicken
- [ ] **Котлеты по киевски** [kotleta po kievski] chicken Kiev*
- [ ] **Плов** [plov] pilaf or pilau
- [ ] **Гарнир** [garnir] side dish: all entrees are served with a side like buckwheat, fried potatoes, cooked cabbage, or veggies

OTHER ZAKUSKI

- [ ] Eggplant caviar
- [ ] Deviled eggs

BREAD

- [ ] White bread
- [ ] Rye bread
- [ ] **Бородинский хлеб** [borodinsky hleb] dark brown rye bread
- [ ] Baguette

*PROVERB ALERT
Горяче? Студи, дураче. [Gorachye? Studi durachye] Too hot? Blow on it you dummy. This is another example of a Ukrainian Russian hybrid phrase..

*FUN FACT
The word for entree in Russian is 'gorachaya' or hot, presumably your entrees are always served hot

*FUN FACT
The spelling of the capital of Ukraine is a topic of debate, some argue that spelling it Kiev is associated with the Russification of Ukraine and the transliteration "Kyiv" was legally mandated by the Ukrainian government in 1995

DESSERT

- ☐ **Наполеон** [Napoleon]
- ☐ **Медовик/ Сметанник** [medovik/smettanik] sour cream cake
- ☐ **Вафельный торт** [vaf-felniy tort] waffle cake

DRINKS ALCOHOLIC

- ☐ Vodka
- ☐ Cognac
- ☐ Champagne

NON ALCOHOLIC BEVERAGES

- ☐ Mineral water*
- ☐ **Квас** [kvas] fermented beverage
- ☐ **Компот** [kompot] fruit beverage
- ☐ **Морс** [mors] lingonberry and cranberry beverage
- ☐ Coffee & Tea- served hot usually with dessert

> ***FUN FACT**
> the Russian Imperial Army discovered the Borjomi mineral springs in 1829, it was widely sold in the Soviet Union and was a top Soviet export

MARINA'S SALAD MASTERPIECES

These salads are elevated depending on the ingredients available to you, particularly the meat used, and can be sized up or down depending on how many people you are feeding. The quantities are estimations as the goal is to balance all of the ingredients. The key to achieving the perfect salad masterpiece a la Marina is to spend time meticulously dicing your ingredients. Each one of my mom's salads has ingredients that are perfectly symmetrical and even in measurement. For many of the salads the measurement of each piece is approximateley 1cm by 1cm.

Салат Оливье
Salat Olivie

Ingredients

3 medium potatoes
2 medium carrots
4 eggs
½ to ⅔ medium onion
2-3 medium pickles
½ to ⅔ lb of meat
4 heaping tbsp mayonnaise
½ can of peas (or ½ cup of fresh)

Instructions

- Boil the veggies in salted water: whole potatoes, carrots until they are fork tender (softness/firmness is a personal preference). Drain and let cool
- Peel veggies once they are cool.
- Hard boil the egg, and peel once cool.
- Cube the boiled veggies (size is a personal preference but recommended 1 cm.)
- Cube the pickles, and onions (make these cubes the smallest.)
- Cube your meat.
- Combine cubed potatoes, carrots, eggs, pickles, onions, meat, add canned peas.
- Add mayonnaise, start with three Tbsp and add more to taste.
- Salt to taste if needed.
- Mix together and serve (or refrigerate.)

Винегрет
Vinaigrette

Ingredients

1 large beet
3 potatoes
1 large carrots
2 pickles
½ onion
⅔ cup pickled cabbage
(homemade or from any Russian or European specialty store)
½ cup canned peas
3 tbsp sunflower oil

Instructions

- Bake or boil beets until fork tender and let cool.
- Boil potatoes and carrots in salted water until fork tender and let cool.
- Once cool, peel potatoes, beets, and carrots.
- Cube potatoes, beets, carrots, pickles, and onion.
- Cut pickled cabbage if pieces are especially large.
- Combine potatoes, carrots, pickles, onion, cabbage, and peas (other options instead of peas are beans.)
- Add sunflower oil, mix well.
- Add salt and sugar to taste.

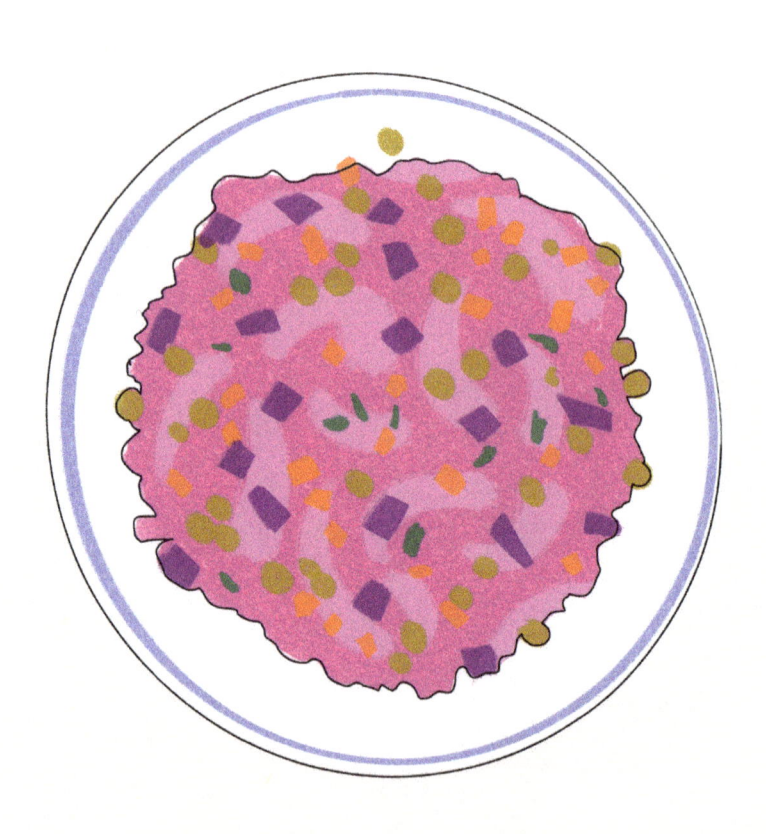

Шуба
Herring Under Fur Coat

Ingredients

1 yellow onion
2 small beets or 1 large
3 potatoes
1 carrot
1 green apple (should be sour)
2 herrings
mayonnaise
(Some people add egg)

Instructions

- Cut onions into half circles, separate into strips and marinate them in vinegar while you prep the remaining ingredients.
- Bake beets until fork tender and let cool.
- Boil carrots and potatoes in salted water until fork tender and let cool
- Once cool, peel and grate beets, potatoes, carrots, and apples. (pro tip: you can also grate each layer directly onto the plate in which you are arranging the salad.)
- You can buy pickled herring that is already deboned, otherwise debone and cube the herring in medium sized cubes.
- Start by arranging roughly half a grated potato as the first thin layer on a plate and layer herring on top
- Optionally layer with mayonnaise or add a little bit of sunflower oil
- Drain the vinegar from the onion and layer marinated onion.
- Layer grated green apple, then layer grated potato.
- Cover with mayonnaise.
  - Layer grated carrot, then layer grated beets.
  - Cover with mayonnaise.
  - Refrigerate ideally for at least twelve hours.
    - Optional: decorate with cubed hard boiled egg and dill when serving.

WHAT YOU CAN MAKE WITH MAYO & EGGS

Mayo + Egg + Garlic = Egg salad or deviled eggs

Mayo + Egg + Garlic + Cheese = Грипозный салат
[gripoznyy salat]

Mayo + Egg + Imitation Crab + Celery + Onion + Cucumber
= Crab salad

Mayo + Egg + Cod Liver in oil + Onion = Салат из печений
трески [salat iz pecheniy treski] cod liver salad

Mayo + Egg + Canned Fish + Carrot + Potato + Onion
= Салат Мимоза [Salat Mimoza]

Новый Год

[Novoi god]

New Year's

Party like it's 1999

This is it, the moment I've been fantasizing about for a millennium! Ok, more like five years... I was eleven years old when I had done the math and calculated that when the clock struck midnight and the calendar leaf flipped over to a whole new year, a new century, a new MILLENIUM! I would be sixteen years old and (where else?) Times Square waiting for the ball to drop with the rest of the revelers.

It never even occurred to me that my parents might not be super into the idea of letting their sixteen-year-old only child travel to New York City by herself. Or that I, at sixteen, had no business being smack dab in the middle of a crowd bigger than fourteen times the population of the small town I grew up in. In my daydream, I didn't even imagine myself surrounded by friends, but realistically, why would I be all by myself in NYC? (Clearly, my fantasy wasn't well thought out.)

Not only did my parents NOT let me go to New York, they wouldn't even let me leave the house! (is added for dramatic effect.)

On December 31st, 1999 while all of my American friends were busy getting dolled up and headed out for various parties all over town (or so I imagine), I had to stay home and play лото* with my grandparents.

This was totally unfair, but also totally expected. Новый Год is after all the biggest family holiday of all.

In the Former Soviet Union, Новый Год* was a government-sanctioned non-religious requirement of revelry.

*DEFINITION
лото [lotto] bingo

*DEFINITION
Новый год [novi god]
New Year's Eve

> ***DEFINITION**
>
> **ёлочка** *[yolachka]* quite literally meant pine tree, the American equivalent is Christmas Tree, or Hanukkah Bush

> ***DEFINITION**
>
> **Дед Мороз** *ded moroz* Grandpa Frost, the American equivalent of this is Santa Claus

> ***DEFINITION**
>
> **Снегурочка** *[snegurachka]* Snowflake. She is Grandpa Frost's granddaughter.

Новый Год (or New Year's Eve) is possibly the defining and enduring tradition of the Soviet era. Новый Год in the Soviet Union evolved from the Christian and pagan traditions of yesteryear with traditions like ёлочка* and gift-giving. After the 1917 Revolution Christmas was outright banned and instead there was a failed attempt to create a communist holiday which (shockingly) did not gain popularity.

By the time Stalin came to power, he reinstated elements of previous celebrations like having a celebratory tree and bringing back Дед Мороз* and this became a civic secular holiday stripped of any (obvious) religious elements. Leading up to the New Year, children in nursery school would put on morning assemblies and plays acting out the story of Grandpa Frost and his granddaughter Снегурочка*, singing songs, and passing out candy to our parents. I am proud to say that one year I was awarded the coveted role in the winter nursery school morning assembly as co-narrator. A role shared with a fellow classmate who had blond hair, as per Soviet school mandate that no potentially Jewish-looking children be given the lead in any school production. (Is meant to be joke, yes?)

For those of us living in [address redacted] Khmelnytskyi, New Year's eve meant a long celebration. We took all the tables we owned, pushed them together in the middle of the living room (also known as Musya and Abram's bedroom), and filled our table to the brim (read: to the best of our abilities) with all the food we could legally (and not so legally) get our hands on and that which we had been stockpiling for at least the last three months.

When we immigrated to America, the tradition of Новый Год, ёлочка, and Дед мороз* came with us. If not in the corporeal form, (we didn't have room in our luggage for any ornaments, for example) but in spirit.

*FUN FACT
note the distinct absence of снегурочка. I guess we left her behind to keep Mother Russia company?

And every December 31st we faithfully recreated the best of the holiday: the food, the games, the drunken toasts, and the handful of presents that magically appeared the next morning from Дед мороз himself, (or my Babushka Liliya, there was never any conclusive proof one way or the other.)

When we celebrated our first New Year's Eve on American soil it was an affair to remember!

But I was eight years old, so I forgot most of it.

I didn't think too hard about Santa Claus and Дед мороз, perhaps they were the same person, perhaps they were different people, either way, I was getting presents so who cares. For the first few years, my parents would coordinate with their group of friends to have an epic celebration and the food was always the focal point. They would decide on a main course and build out a menu from there. There were color-coded menu plans and one show-stopping entree after another—one year was [insert fancy restaurant style description] piglet, another—cheese stuffed lobsters. Of the thirty years we have lived in America, my parents only broke with tradition a handful of times to celebrate with friends instead of family because ~~personal freedoms are a ridiculous American concept~~ my Babushka's wishes to spend all subsequent New Years Eves as a family prevailed.

One of our first few parties/gatherings

Your Soviet New Year's Eve Checklist

Here's how you can plan your very own Soviet inspired NYE celebration: [Food and drink, decor, music, games and activities, bonus points: the day after]

Start with the special occasions mix and match AND add the following:

- Champagne* for the midnight toast
- Bonus points if you can work in the upcoming animal from the Chinese zodiac (this does not mean cook a rooster for the Year of the Rooster, it means have a creative interpretation of how you can bring that animal's presence forward in the dishes served
- Non-negotiable must haves for New Year's Eve – every family has their own NYE must haves. Ours are:
    - ✦ Блинчики [blinchiki] crepes
    - ✦ Салат Оливье [salat olivye] salad Olivye
    - ✦ Селёдка с картошкой [seledka s kartoshkoi] pickled herring and mashed potatoes*
    - ✦ Винегрет [vinegret] salad Vinegret
    - ✦ Холодное [holodnoye] aspic

The key to a successful New Year's Eve menu is getting the quantity right. You have to have enough courses to make it to midnight (and beyond) AND have plenty leftover for New Year's Day.

> *NOW & THEN
>
> Советское шампанское [Sovetskoye Shampanskoye] Soviet Champagne ais the champagne of Soviet champions. It was produced in the Soviet Union and after the collapse several private companies bought the right to use it.

> *FUN FACT
>
> Pickled herring and potatoes are a requirement for any of our family gatherings and my parents often remark that this is the only thing they need for culinary happiness.

CLOTHES

At some point, a secret think tank issues a recommendation for the appropriate color that you must include in your NYE ensemble.

It's tradition to wear something brand new on New Year's Eve (yes, underwear counts). Some wear only new things on NYEs.

Getting dressed up is an enduring tradition.

*THEN & NOW

Soviet ornaments had a few distinct themes: characters from fairy tales, people of various professions, fruits & vegetables, family life and prosperity, clocks, rockets cosmonaut and space themes as well as military such as the Soviet star and the hammer and sickle were popular. In America my family's tradition is to buy an ornament a year to represent something meaningful that happened that year.

New Year's

DECOR

- ☐ The **ёлочка** [elochka] Christmas Tree* with ornaments to boot!
- ☐ The top of the tree is decorated with a star*.
- ☐ **Дождик** [dozhdik] which translates to "light rain" but is actually tinsel and is positively non-negotiable.
- ☐ **Огоньки** [ogonki] lights.
- ☐ **Гирлянды** [girlandi] garlands which could also be lights but can also mean ropes of decorations that go around the tree
- ☐ Bengali lights or sparklers for the brave among you
- ☐ Noisemakers of all kinds

*FUN FACT

We used to get our Christmas trees for free right after Christmas, until the tree sellers wised up

GAMES/ACTIVITIES

Лото [lotto] Bingo Rummikub- an Israeli tile based game that combined elements of rummi and mahjong

Chess- no one escapes learning how to play chess in a Soviet or Soviet immigrant household

Cards- a popular game is дурак [durak] which means fool.

*THEN & NOW

Soviet tree toppers were often the red star with the hammer and sickle. Here we are content with any star shape.

MOVIES

Classic Soviet New Year's Eve movies include:
Ирония судьбы или с лёгким паром [ironiya sudbi ili s lekhim parom] this long winded movie title translates to 'The irony of fate, or enjoy your bath.' This is technically a romantic comedy but as with all Soviet films* this love story is seeped in sadness.

*FUN FACT
My aunt & uncle watch this movie every New Year's Eve without fail!

Карнавальная ночь [karnavalnaya noch] Carnival night. This 1956 musical is set on New Year's Eve with the employees of the House of Culture set to perform their New Year's Eve variety show when a new director threatens to change it all.

Бриллиантовая Рука [brillantovaya ruka] The Diamond Arm. If you're in the mood for something different, this lighthearted crime comedy (considered by many to be the best comedic Soviet film of all time) about smugglers who try to transport jewels in an orthopedic cast worn by un unsuspecting man in the wrong time and wrong place will do the trick.

MUSIC

Our family tradition in the Soviet Union was watching Новогодний Голубой огонек [Novogodniy Goluboy ogonyok] New Year's Eve Blue Light*, the first Soviet entertainment show. You can catch re-reruns on YouTube! More often than not a good NYE party involves someone busting out the guitar and everyone singing along to some Soviet classics.

*PROVERB ALERT

This show was named in part for the light blue glare of the TV screen and in part for the concept of friendly visits: **заглянуть на огонек** [zaglyanut na ogonyok] – to look in on a light, or to visit someone unannounced (after seeing a light in their window)

THE DAY AFTER

Not unlike the post-wedding brunch the next day our NYE tradition includes getting together a mere 10 hours later to finish eating all of the food. A nice contrast to all of the stress of planning the perfect New Year's Eve, the day after is a more casual, relaxed affair that can last into the evening.

Remix/Dejavu - What is Старый Новый Год [stariy novoi god] Old New Years?

An adorable oxymoron stemming from the fact that in 1917 the Soviet Union moved to the Gregorian calendar, but because the Russian Orthodox Church uses the Julian calendar, New Year's comes two weeks later. And this means you get to celebrate twice! This was also a way to ostensibly celebrate Christmas since the Christmas holidays were decoupled from New Year's.

Холодец
Babushka Liliya's Holodetz (aka Aspic)

Ingredients

4lbs leg of beef
1 ox tail
2 beef shanks
4 chicken legs
(drumsticks and thighs)
1 onion
1-2 carrots
1-3 bay leaves
garlic

Instructions

- Bring beef leg and ox tail to a boil, remove and wash the leg under cold water, then put the meat back in a large pot.
- Bring beef shanks to a boil, remove and wash the shanks under cold water, then add to beef leg and ox tail.
- Bring chicken legs to a boil, remove and wash the chicken legs under cold water, and add to the rest of the meat.
- Pour enough water into the pot so that it covers the meat and another 1-2 inches beyond that.
- Bring to a boil, remove any foam, reduce heat to simmer.
- While it's simmering add a mostly peeled onion, bay leaf, salt, carrots, and whole peppercorns.
- Remove chicken legs once they are cooked, and debone and remove skin.
- Remove the rest from heat once gelatin can be easily removed from the beef bones (1-2 hours.)
- Cut carrots into circles.
- Take a deep plate, add salt, and grate a garlic clove to create a paste that you spread around the bottom of the plate, add chicken meat or beef meat, mix meat with garlic, add the broth to cover the meat, add carrot circles and put in the refrigerator until it sets (at least four hours).
- Serve with horseradish, spicy mustard, or your favorite condiment.

Babushka Liliya's Блинчики Blinchiki (crepes)

Makes 45 Blinchiki, to feed a family of 12 at least once

Ingredients

1 cup flour
pinch of salt
1 tsp sugar
4 eggs
½ cup lukewarm water
1-1 ½ cup lukewarm milk
2 tbsp vegetable oil

Instructions

- Combine flour, salt, and sugar.
- Beat eggs and add to dry ingredients and stir to combine.
- Heat ½ cup of water until lukewarm and using a hand mixer gradually combine with batter until no lumps remain.
- Heat ½ cup of milk until warm, gradually add to batter, using hand mixer to combine
- Add more milk if needed, the mixture should be somewhat runny.
- Grease a crepe pan with vegetable oil and heat up.
- Once the pan is warm add a ladleful to the center of the pan and gently rotate the pan to spread the batter thinly and evenly.
- Flip the crepe once you see bubbles and that the edges are forming.
- Taste the first crepe, and if it's too thick add more milk to the batter.
- Once you're satisfied with the crepe consistency and taste, keep frying more crepes.

Serve warm or store in the refrigerator until needed. If refrigerating, Babushka's recommendation is to wrap the blinchiki in a paper towel and then in aluminum foil and then put in a plastic bag.

Свадьба

[Svadba]

Wedding

First comes love then comes marriage

(Unless you're in the Soviet Union where there's no access to legal and safe abortion and practically no access to contraceptives*. Then sometime comes an accidental pregnancy then marriage. Love is optional.)

> *FUN FACT
>
> a comical cognate is the word **презерватив** [preservative] which means condom in Russian (not jam)

"Have you ever been to American Wedding? Where's the vodka? Where's the pickled herring?"

GOGOL BORDELLO

Weddings are about a lot of things—the celebration of love, the coming together of families, and of course, the food and drink!

But before we make it to the wedding let's chat about the Soviet concept of dating according to my babushka, of ухаживать* [uhazhivanya] What is uhazhivat? It means to take care of a woman.

> *FUN FACT
>
> in a non-dating context **ухаживать** still means to take care of someone. For example, while sharing a meal together one person might take care of another by putting food on their plate or making sure they have a water glass.

Allow babushka to share her love story to illustrate this concept:

Me: How did you meet дедушка [dedushka*]?

Babushka: In school.

M: What grade were you in?

B: 7th, he was in 8th.

M: What was it like? Were you immediately smitten with each other?

B: It was school days. We had a group of friends and we went to dances, evening hangouts, the movies, there was hugging kissing, etc.

And then when I went away to school in Львов [Lvov], and he went to Харьков [Kharkov]...

> ***DEFINITION**
>
> if you guessed this means grandfather you are correct! Take a cookie off the shelf!

And now a short tangent into antisemitism in the Soviet Union...

M: What did you study?

B: Elcectrotechnical communications.

M: Why that specifically?

B: No one else took me.

M: Why?

B: Because of the пятая графа [pyatoya grafa]

M: What is that?

B: It's the fifth line of your passport application:

last name

first name

patronym*

date of birth

ethnicity

Your ethnicity was listed as Jewish* and you were essentially denied admission anywhere. You had to be the best of the best or you had to pay someone off.

> ***FUN FACT**
>
> a patronym takes your father's name and adds an ending to it to denote "son of" or "daughter of." For example my husband is Stanislav and his father is Oleg, add "ovich" to Oleg and you get Stanislav Olegovich. My name is Yuliya and my dad is Peter, so my patronym is Petrovna. Patronyms were used in official documents and when addressing someone both formally and informally.

> ***FUN FACT**
>
> despite being born in the Ukraine our ethnicity was still listed as Jewish (not Ukranian)

Back to our regularly scheduled programming....

> M: Was he the only person you were dating?
>
> B: No I was friendly with other boys—дружила [druzhila]
>
> M: What is the difference between friendly дружить [druzhit] and dating встречаться [vstrechatsa]?
>
> B: Well with him we were already dating and everyone knew we were a pair.
>
> M: When did you date Garik? (Her sister's husband)
>
> B: I never dated him! He came into my life and I introduced him to my sister.
>
> (How very Shakespearean)
>
> M: Why did you like my grandpa then?
>
> B: He was smart, studied hard, played sports, wrote poetry, did handwork. And all the holidays we would get together in a group of friends компания [kompaniya]... we were 14, 15, 16.
>
> M: Where did you have these parties?
>
> B: At people's houses and when we got together the boys would buy wine, vodka
>
> M: Wow!
>
> B: When we were all together other boys sometimes ухаживали за мной [uhazhivaly za mnoi] took care of me.
>
> M: What does that mean?
>
> B: It means paying special attention, buying me flowers, walking me home after school, asking me to dance, but I only had eyes for him.

And there you have ladies and gentlemen, when you are dating the man takes care of you and once you're married you have the esteemed pleasure of taking care of him. For life.

MEMORIES, MEMENTOS & MENUS

Family Weddings

Wedding of Tanya and Vladimer, from left to right Baba Lilliya, Baba Musya, Deda Abram, Mom Marina, Bride Tanya (Deda Vova's sister) and Groom Vladimer (Vova's Brother in Law)

Author's Father and Mother in Law– Yelena and Oleg

Author's maternal grandparents wedding

American Soviet Style Wedding Menu

Blintzes with black caviar
Smoked Fish Platter
Pickled Platter
Khachapuri
Eel Salad with Seaweed and Mixed Greens
Ahi Tuna salad
Farmers' salad
Blintzes with meat and mushroom sauce
Poached Sturgeon
Roasted Potatoes with Porcini
Shish kabob
Vodka
Cognac
Champagne
Wine
Opera Cake

Author's maternal grandparents wedding

Parents official wedding portraits

Author's parents Peter & Marina

Soviet Menu

Herring
Potatoes mashed
Salteson (kishka stuffed with meat)
Aspic
Olivie
Vinaigrette
Buzhenina
Kielbasa
Sprats
Vodka
Sitro
Champagne
Zharkoye main course
Korolevski tort

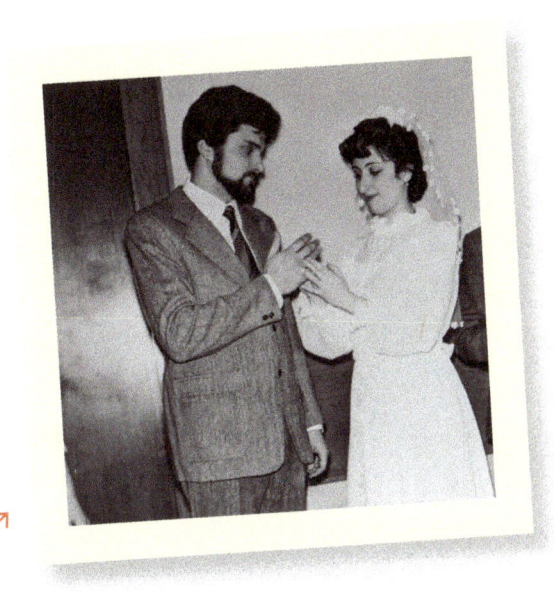

BUT FIRST? FIRST, THERE WAS "US."

> ***FUN FACT**
> this is a **HOHMA** - a joke or a funny, witty tale

And before we were an "us," we were just two people. Two very hungover people hobbling together towards the nearest Starbucks off frat row on University Avenue...

Insipid sunshine searing into my retinas. Temples pounding, stomach churning, even my skin hurts.

GAWD, why did I drink so much? I will never, ever, for as long as I live drink alcohol ever again. Ever... I could really go for a Jack in the Crack breakfast sandwich, but that is too damn far to walk.

He hands me a bottle and reminds me to drink.

WATER!!!

He reminds me to drink water because neither one of us is ever drinking alcohol ever, again.

Ever.

The smell of coffee hits my nostrils, my Pavlovian response kicks in and I summon strength I didn't even know I had to drag my limbs onward and inside the mothership.

"Grande, non-fat hazelnut latte and a small coffee, room for cream please." *But since he's paying, maybe I should get a muffin too...*

We slump into chairs (which smell the way only Starbucks chairs this close to campus could smell) and try to appear nonchalant.

Riiight. Damn this is awkward. A month ago he was just this nerdy guy... and now? Well hell if I know, I think he could be "the one," but I've been wrong before.

A jazz melody begins to play. Softly, thank God.

"I see trees of green, red roses too..."

Dude. I know that song. I'm about to impress the hell out of him, he looks sensitive enough to like jazz.

"Oh. I just loove Duke Ellington."

Silence.

He blinks excessively (which is annoying)

"I'm pretty sure that's Louis Armstrong."

"What*ever*. I'm pretty sure that I *know* jazz and I'm pretty sure that's Duke Ellington."

He shrugs.

Wise move buddy. Don't argue with me. I'm hungover and I'm always right.

His breathing sounds argumentative* and I will not stand for it!

"Fine, I'll prove it to you" I stomp off to the counter.

"Excuse me," *bubbly blonde barista chick,* "who's this song by?"

"Oh it's Louis Armstrong!"

Dammit.

Now what the hell do I do? I look at him, he looks at me. This is it, the moment of truth.

His eyes crinkle as he smiles. He looks so damn goofy with that smile, and I know what I have to do.

"Attention people of Starbucks! This man right here, see him? Wave hello to the nice people of Starbucks. He was RIGHT and I was WRONG, I just needed you ALL to know that."

I take a bow and accept my applause.

Years later, as I walk down the aisle to the gravelly, unmistakable voice of none other than Louis Armstrong, I know this for sure, I may have been wrong about that song, but I was right about him.

*FUN FACT

"Chill honey bunny" - what my husband says to me these days instead of *"calm down"*- which as every sane person knows are fighting words

Our Wedding

Setting romance aside for a moment and putting tradition on a neat little box on the shelf, I have to confess that before my fellow former Soviet fella and I had our wedding, we had to get legally married, under a shroud of secrecy in a nondescript courtroom in Reno.

IF YOU WANT TO MARRY YOUR COUSIN, DON'T COME TO RENO, NV.

*FUN FACT
this story is a **MANTSA** or a bit of juicy gossip

It's a tale as old as time: girl meets boy, boy loves girl, girl's health insurance runs out, and boy has to legally wed her to provide her with the important things in life: an HMO/major medical.

I remember the day (but ironically, not the date) like it was yesterday…I was finishing up a client meeting in a downtown Reno Starbucks waiting for my 'fiance' to show up so we could hop on over to the courthouse and sign some papers granting us both the piece of mind of legally adding me to his health insurance.

We were running out of time as this was the last day that I legally had my own insurance, and back then, we, okay, I, really got my rocks off on dancing right on the edge of a deadline. That or I was slightly scatterbrained and doing a million other things trying to get my first business off the ground, or I was so in love it made me delirious and stupid…yeah yeah it was definitely the love thing!

(Love ya honey, thanks for putting up with me all these years!)

So…where was I… Oh yeah scatterbrained and delinquent! And now with fiancé in tow on our way over to the courthouse.

But… oh no… what's this?

The bag I grabbed this morning apparently only has my debit card, some questionable trail mix, an expired student ID, and nothing in the way of official government identification!

There's no time to head back home (thirty minutes away) to get the appropriate documents, the courthouse closes at 5, and did I mention this is the last day I have health insurance? If I can't be trusted to remember my wallet then I definitely can't be trusted to wander out into the world without an insurance safety net!

I say we take a chance and go to the courthouse, this is Reno, after all, the town of the quickie marriage and even quicker divorce.

As we sheepishly stand, hand in hand, I explain our (my) situation to the [insert vague description of a civil servant of the feminine persuasion at the courthouse here] 18 minutes away from the end of her shift.

She looks at us, eyes narrowed, and asks,

"Are y'all over 18?"

We shake our heads in assent. Yes, ma'am.

"Are y'all cousins?"

Gulp (I resist every single urge to make a joke). No, ma'am, we're not cousins.

"Alright, go on in then," and she waved us toward the next set of doors.

I truly have no idea what happened next. We repeated some words, signed some papers, gave a vial of blood, and submitted a urine sample… wait no, I might be confusing this story with another one.

We drove home as "husband and wife" and didn't tell a soul except our Rabbi. And because she was (and is) an amazing human being, she just shrugged and said, "It's fine. I'll just fudge the legal language in the ceremony. No one will ever even notice."

She was right.

No one noticed because they were too busy having the time of their lives at our wedding.

It was an epic wedding, if I do say so myself.

WEDDING TRADITIONS: YOURS, MINE, AND OURS

People assume that the bride is the most difficult player in a wedding (a bridezilla, as you may have heard her referred to colloquially), but there are usually several people vying for the title of biggest pain in the tuchus*, some you'd never even expect. Your childhood best friend, for example, one of seven bridesmaids, insists that she couldn't possibly wear a gold bridesmaid dress because the color makes her look fat. Not the cut of the dress or the material (or even the size of the gown!) but the actual color GOLD is to blame for this feeling of fatness.

> ***DEFINITION**
>
> tuchus is Yiddish for butt, a favorite expression of mine is 'Kishen Tuchus' which translates to kiss my a$$

Having been a wedding planner for four years, at the time I planned my own, I was pretty familiar with the production that is a wedding. I knew that the hardest part was not the logistics of figuring out how to get a rented stove to the third floor of a building with an elevator that belonged in a museum (or the setting of a murder mystery.)

I knew that the hardest part was the people management of it all.

The delicate balance of meeting the needs and desires of all of the key people involved in wedding planning.

Our caterer, for instance, with whom menu planning went something like this.

Us: We'd like this item on your catering menu for our wedding

Her: This is what you want? No, this is not what you want. Let me tell you what you want!*

> ***FUN FACT**
>
> this is but one example of the charm of Soviet customer service

My mother (and granted, mothers are a very predictable choice for most difficult member of the wedding party) and her irrational insistence on a "broth course" - that's hot broth served to drunk wedding guests, and her equally unreasonable attachment to serving individually plated entrees!

Please picture a table laden with so many appetizers that some threaten to actually fall off the table and then imagine eating an individually plated entree on top of all this food.

I knew my guests couldn't handle it. They might be mostly former Soviet folks but they weren't bears coming out of hibernation. I knew this food would be wasted and I stood my ground forcing my mom to pick several other battles to wage.

Of course, we didn't do ourselves any favors by making our wedding theater themed allowing for obvious theater tropes and roles to emerge:

- the ingenue: the bride
- the cruel and unrelenting director: the bride (and also TBH the mother of the bride)
- the producers: people who foot part of the bill and insist their demands for extra guests be met
- the supporting cast: our bridesmaids and groomsmen and there were twelve of them....so... extra drama!
- bit players with an inflated sense of ego: I won't name names but you know who you were
- the talent: in our case both the actual wedding band and special guest singer, a one Gennadiy Visotskiy (no relation)*, and my mom, dad, aunt and uncle, grandma, grandpa and niece who created a special performance where they took Russian songs that were popular and re-wrote the lyrics to tell the story of our lives!
- the villain: again I won't name names but our caterer certainly springs to mind
- the audience: our wedding guests who were each an integral part of our wedding/theatrical performance

> *FUN FACT
>
> Владимир Высоцкий [Vladimir Visotskiy] was a Soviet singer-songwriter, poet, and actor. Immensely popular and remembered for this unique singing style.

In true theatrical fashion we did things like time the food courses to the music - we asked our caterer to serve stuffed fish (gefilte fish) just as my dad sang a Yiddish ballad—секрет фаршированной рыбы [sekret farshorivonay ribye] the secret of stuffed fish*.

My dad also emceed the entire event because I simply didn't trust anyone else to do the job. But demanding that my dad spend the entire wedding of his only child entertaining guests wasn't very bridezilla of me, was it?

My *coughs meaningfully*...one and only bridezilla moment was about cake.

I had never had wedding cake that I actually enjoyed and was convinced the whole tradition was irrelevant. So I demanded a chocolate fountain!

By this point, our wedding budget had inflated to a number that would have been enough to use as a down payment on a house, so I bartered for the fountain and invited an acquaintance to the wedding in exchange for the retail cost of the fountain.

In the end, I got my chocolate fountain and the guests got a crash course in Soviet-style weddings. If you should ever find yourself at one here are some helpful tips!

> ***FUN FACT**
>
> what is the secret to stuffed fish (or gefilte fish)? According to Soviet (and Jewish!) poet and song writer Mikhail Tanich the secret was **Сперва фаршируется рыба, Гостей приглашают потом!** -First you stuff the fish, then (and only then) you invite the guests.

Wedding tidbits

- Some of the mystifying traditions happen before the wedding. Traditions include: holding the bride for ransom until the groom has paid for her, which most likely comes from the tradition of dowry.
- A Jewish wedding has several distinct rituals: the ketubah (marriage contract) signing, the ceremony, yichud - the quiet moment for the bride and groom (pretty sure the intent for this was to consummate the marriage), and the reception.
- Weddings were a symbol of capitalism therefore, from 1917 through the mid-1930s the Soviets discouraged people from getting married.
- Many cultural traditions were religious ones, therefore they were essentially outlawed during Soviet time.
- Комсомольская свадьба* [komsomolskaya svadba] essentially a civil wedding where members of the Komsomol would go to the bureau and give speeches to the bride and groom.
- To gift or not to gift? Hot tip: what the bride and groom want most is cash money.
- Because most people in the Soviet Union didn't have cameras/video cameras for weddings and special occasions, you would go to a studio to take wedding portraits.

> *DEFINITION
>
> Komsomol is a syllabic abbreviation of the political youth organization in the Soviet Union- **Коммунистический Союз Молодёжи** [Kommunisticheskiy Soyuz Molodyozhi]

If you find yourself at an American Russian/Jewish wedding, please don't be alarmed by the following:

- No bars - cash, hosted or otherwise! But Vodka (cognac and wine) will be placed right on the table so please to enjoy! Select the least intoxicated person to pour for everyone (or the MOST intoxicated, that's a whole other kind of fun!)
- There will be a minimum of Twenty-seven toasts (but if you're keeping up with one shot per toast you won't mind after the third!)
- After every toast is given, chances are high that a chorus of Горько! [gorko] will ring out. At which the newlyweds are supposed to kiss. The literal translation of this word is "bitter!" and there are many theories as to why this is shouted at the couple. One possibility is that the bitterness of vodka is supposed to be offset by the kiss of the bride and groom.
- The chair throwing or chair dance where the bride and groom are placed on chairs hoisted in the air and carried around by friends and family. Some traditions* include the bride and groom holding on to a piece of fabric hoisted in chairs.
- A tamada*/emcee/toastmaster/master of ceremonies. Guests must be entertained all night long and this person's job is to keep everyone on the right track and introduce those giving toasts.
- The schedule: toast/drink/eat/dance repeat.
- The challah pull (who wears the pants in the family): similar to the wishbone at an American Thanksgiving, the couple pulls at two sides of the challah and whoever ends up with the bigger half is the boss!
- The most important part is you must give money as a gift.

---

*NOW & THEN

This evolved from Orthodox and conservative weddings where men and women were separated by a curtain (a mechitza) and hoisting the bride and groom in chairs gave them an opportunity to "dance" with one another. These days we do it because it makes for hilarious photos.

*FUN FACT

the name 'tamada' comes from the Georgian republic and means master of ceremonies. Other Soviet republics might have referred to this person as **свадебный генерал** *[svadebniy general] or wedding general.*

День рождения
[Den rozhdeniya]
Birthday

What sets birthdays apart from every other kind of special occasion? I would have to say it's definitely the cake.

My most memorable birthday would have to be... all of them. I love birthdays and I would be surprised if any don't top the list even if they were objectively terrible (21st birthday and 13th birthday I'm looking at you.)

But of course, for me, my birthdays were the most significant when I was a child. Not necessarily because of presents, because I only recall three birthdays when presents made any impression on me (my seventh, sixth, and fifth), but because for a brief moment in time, the spotlight was on me! Not every child enjoys this but you can probably guess that I sure took advantage of every second of being center stage.

But wait, birthday presents? Let's review the top three best presents I got as a child:

1. Красная коляска [krasnaya kolyaska] red stroller - a real stroller that I used for my dolls that was later handed down and used as an actual stroller for my second cousin Masha.
2. Буратино и малвина [buratino and malvina] - two dolls based on the Russian version of Pinocchio*. Buratino derives from the Italian word for wooden puppet. Malvina is the fairy with turquoise hair that rescues Buratino from some mishaps. My friend Svetlana managed to break the legs off of my Malvi-

*FUN FACT

In this version of Pinocchio a sad puppet named Pierrot is in love with Malvina, He is a poet and his melancholy poetry is featured in the book, a very typical Soviet sadness in a story for children.

na, and I, being the bigger person at seven years old, immediately forgave her and never brought it up again. Certainly not at her wedding. And certainly not in a book for all to see.
3. Гоша [Gosha] the marionette—I saved the best for last.....read on if you dare...

Now, this is an odd story that brings us to the counterpoint of birthdays: death. The night before I was to turn seven years old I stayed out late (past sunset!) with the neighborhood kids.

We lived in a multi-story apartment complex surrounded by other multi-story apartments, and in the middle of these apartments was an open space with a garden, benches, and a gazebo.

So the neighborhood ~~hooligans~~ children and I gathered to tell ghost stories after dark in the gazebo. I was the youngest there and the older kids made it their mission to scare the wits out of me.

They told me the most terrifying story of a coffin on wheels that follows people around warning them of their impending death. I barely ran home without peeing myself from fear.

The very next morning my parents, who were completely unaware of the events of the previous night, planned a birthday surprise for me. I woke up to the sound of a door creaking and the sight of an unidentified creature creeping into my room.

I screamed a blood-curdling scream, startling and confusing my parents who yelled for me to calm down. It turned out that they had bought a special marionette dragon doll for me and were controlling it from behind the door frame. I named the marionette Gosha and he was my best buddy until we had to leave him (and the rest of my possessions) behind when we immigrated.

(Note what is absent from this list of top birthday gifts: Barbies—what a disappointment...and a story for another book)

THE FiVE BEST BiRTHDAY CAKES COUNTDOWN

#5 Наполеон [Napoleon] Napoleon cake is said to be inspired by a classic mille-feuille (French for "thousand leaves" because of its many layers) and it's made with multiple thin layers of puffed pastry and pastry cream or custard. I may be the only former Soviet person who is lukewarm about this cake. I mean I'll eat it, it IS cake afterall, but I'm not begging my mom to make it when there are so many other cakes in the world to choose from.

#4 Киевский [Kyivskyi] - two layers of meringue with hazelnuts, chocolate glaze, and a buttercream-like filling. This cake was first made at the Karl Marx confectionary factory in 1956 and became super popular all over the Soviet Union.

#3 Павлова [Pavlova*] - not technically cake and more of a cake-like circular chunk of baked meringue, with a crisp crust and soft, light inside, usually topped with fruit like strawberries or raspberries and whipped cream. It is believed to be named for the ballerina Anna Pavlova.

> ***FUN FACT**
> Russian speakers pronounce this cake PA-vlova and Americans pronounce it pa-VLO-va

#2 Вафельный [vafel'nyy] waffle - everyone else in the world apparently made this cake with waffles and condensed milk, but our family did not (see recipe below). This is the cake I most associate with birthdays.

> ***FUN FACT**
> there are passionate debates as to whether this cake's true name is **сметаник** [smettanik] sour cream cake or **медовик** [medovik] honey cake. Either way it's delicious. Have a piece and stop arguing.

#1 Сметанник [smetannik] sour cream cake - nine or ten thin layers with a sour cream filling. I first remember trying this when my then boyfriend's (now husband's) mother made it for a birthday. And this cake might have been what sealed the deal. Or love. Could have been love.

Мечта My Mother in Law's Mechta

Ingredients

Cake layers:

4 tbsp (60g) butter, room temperature
1 cup sugar
2 tbsp honey
2 tbsp vodka
3 eggs, beaten
flour 2 cups and 1 ½ cups
2 level tsp baking soda

Cake filling:

3lbs sour cream*
1 cup sugar
2 cups finely ground walnuts
1-2 tsps vanilla

*NOW & THEN

this recipe started out as 3 cups of sour cream but over the years as I was served this cake I kept wishing it had more cream until 20 years later my mother in law now uses 3lbs of sour cream to make me happy!

For cake dough:

- Preheat oven 375F
- In a double boiler, mix butter with sugar, stirring constantly for 5 minutes.
- Remove from heat, add honey and vodka, and return to double boiler for 3 minutes.
- Remove from heat, allow to cool slightly, add three beaten eggs.
- Sift 2 cups of flour and 2 tsp of baking soda, add to mixture.
- Return to double boiler and stir constantly for 3 minutes.
- Remove and allow to cool, add remaining 1 ½ cups of flour.
- Mix thoroughly so that all flour is incorporated.
- Sprinkle flour on board so that dough doesn't stick, lightly knead the dough, shape into a log and cut into 8-10 even pieces.
- Put back into mixing bowl, cover with a towel and place back into the double boiler that is turned off but still warm.
- Take one piece at a time and flatten with rolling pin until very, very thin approximately ¼ of a centimeter.
- Dock all over with a fork and put on a parchment paper or silicone pad on a baking sheet.
- Bake until golden brown (time varies but you can aim for 6-7 minutes.)
- While one is baking roll out the next, and so on until all 8-10 pieces have been baked
- As each layer is finished cut into a circle while

still warm (about 10" in diameter; suggestion: use a plate about the size you want; place plate on top and cut around it),
- Grind the scraps in a food processor and set aside to use as a crumb layer.

For filling:

- Use standing mixer or handheld mixer to whip sour cream while gradually mixing in sugar, don't overwhip.
- Add vanilla.

To arrange:

- Take a layer and using a big spoon add the filling to the top and spread evenly.
- Sprinkle finely ground walnuts.
- Repeat with each layer.
- When you finish the last layer, cover the sides of the cake with the remaining filling, Cover with a crumb layer on top and sides.
- Cover and leave in refrigerator for at least 24 hours before serving.

Вафельный торт
Waffle Cake

Ingredients

1 package plain wafers – round or square (9 layers, 9-inch diameter) - you can purchase these in any Russian/European store

1¼ cups (200g) honey

⅔ cups (150g) sugar

1 cup coarsely chopped walnuts

2 tbsp cacao

8 oz (200 g) unsalted butter

¼ lemon juiced

Instructions

- In a pan melt butter, then add honey, butter, sugar, stirring frequently and bring to a boil
- Once it's brought to a boil, add walnuts, mix for about a minute, add cacao, mix until everything is combined and there are no lumps.
- Remove from heat and add lemon juice.
- Taste it and add more lemon if needed.
- Put a waffle down and scoop some filing.
- Layer a second waffle and pat strongly.
- After the last waffle layer add a weight on top (a 3L bottle of pickles for example!)
- Let sit overnight at least, then cut and serve.

BIRTHDAYS: THERE, THEN, NOW

What is a birthday tradition for one family is not necessarily tradition for another. My dad, for example, had never celebrated his birthday prior to joining my mom's family. It is through them that he discovered that birthdays are a mandatory celebration of you and attended by your whole family.

Speaking of traditions, birthday cards weren't really a thing. They weren't sold in stores, and while some made them by hand it wasn't a popular Soviet custom—unlike flowers! For a birthday greeting, flowers were a must!

Beyond wishing the birthday recipient a happy birthday, we had (and continue to uphold) the tradition of celebrating everyone in connection with the birthday person with the greeting of с именинником [s immeninikom] that essentially translates to "I congratulate you on the birth of the special person close to you whose birthday it is." It is customary to wish this to the parents, siblings, grandparents, a spouse, a child, really anyone who has a connection to the birthday person. It's a nice reminder that we do not exist on our own but are part of a family, a community, a collective...of socialist republics.

And finally, not all birthdays are created equal. You have your regular birthdays - two, nine, forty eight, etc and your anniversary birthdays юбилей [yubiley] 10, 15, 25, etc.

In the former Soviet Union the most important birthday was arguably your 16th, it is when you became a Soviet Citizen, were issued a passport, could legally drink, get married, and in just two short years you could get drafted into the army! Surely a reason to celebrate.

Regret. You are a ten-year-old's unsophisticated palate.

My family and I happened to be spending my 10th birthday during our first real vacation in America. On the beautiful island of Hawaii. My parents spent the days ~~sneaking food from the complementary breakfast buffet~~ tanning and swimming and I spent my days diving into waves, devouring pineapple and the Joy Luck Club.

In an unprecedented move, on my birthday, my parents let me be the birthday queen by granting me the authority to pick where we would all have my birthday dinner.

I could have selected any place I wanted: sushi, Chinese food, a traditional Hawaiian luau...

What did I pick with almost every international offering available to me?

Denny's.

I picked Denny's.

It represented the epitome of all of my assimilation desires.

It is something I regret to this very day.

And I drown my regrets with as much sushi as humanly possible. Birthday or not.

For contrast here is my oldest daughter's wishes for her tenth birthday party menu: Appetizers: sashimi, mashed potatoes, ceasar salad, bread with caviar, pickled tomatoes. Main course: pasta with stew. Soup: kapustnyak. Dessert: Mechta, Kievski Cake, and Poppyseed Roll.

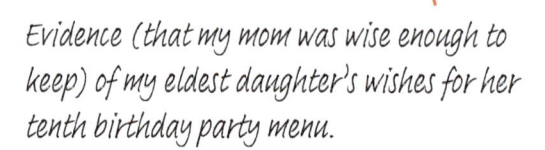

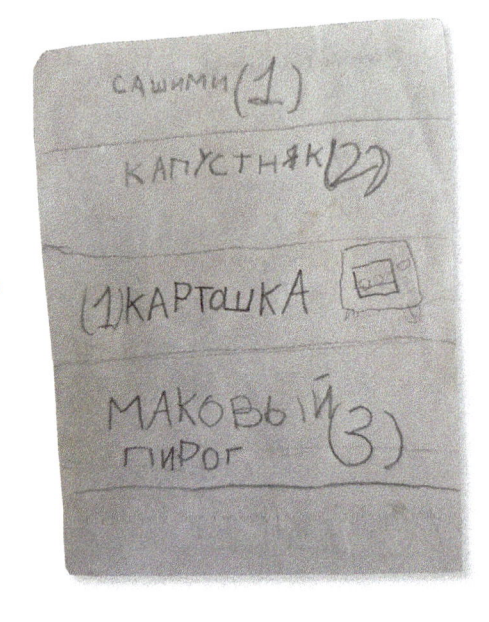

Evidence (that my mom was wise enough to keep) of my eldest daughter's wishes for her tenth birthday party menu.

Acceptable ways to greet the (former Soviet) birthday person:

BEST: A social media greeting in conjunction with a phone call during which you must speak to the birthday person (or leave a voicemail) or it doesn't count. And then as discussed you must wish all of the relatives* of the birthday person a hearty congratulations.

SECOND BEST: By phone (this may result in an invite to a casual celebration that day!)

THIRD BEST: Voicemail

FOURTH BEST: Text

FIFTH BEST: Social media

> *FUN FACT
>
> This is only relevant for those closest to you, so my aunt for example should call my mom on my birthday to wish my mom congratulations on my birth. Friends are usually spared these prescriptions, but it's always a nice touch if friends call too!

You must shower the birthday person with greetings, flowers, time together, well-thought toasts perhaps written on a birthday card so that you have the special memory forever.

Top tips for birthday ~~roasts~~ toasts:

- To drink, a toast must always be said first.
- Ensure you have a закуска [zakuska] an appetizer chaser to help the alcohol go down.
- Don't drink between toasts. Or at least be subtle about it.
- During the reign of Stalin the first toast had to be said in his honor and in honor of the communist party. This was done without fail, for you never knew who might rat you out to the KGB for NOT raising your first toast in honor of Stalin and therefore openly criticizing the state. We no longer say

the first toast to the communist party but we do always say a toast to America at some point.
- Traditionally, the first three toasts are said in honor of the birthday person, followed by toasts in honor of the spouse, parents, grandparents, other family and friends.
- Toasts are often said in order of seniority (oldest family members go first), but it's a complicated balancing act between oldest family members, those closest to the birthday person, and those that have known the birthday person longest.
- It's typically considered bad form for someone to give a second toast before someone else has had the chance to give a first. So get your life together when your turn comes because you may not get another opportunity to speak.
- When in doubt you can offer to toast to health за здоровье [za zdorovye]
- My dad's tradition is always to say a third toast for the ladies. He claims this is a tradition started in Tsarist Russia.
- Often, a toast is said for those no longer with us - but you don't clink glasses for for it.
- Kids can participate in the fun by clinking glasses filled with non alcoholic beverages or in our family we tap the nose of the child instead of clinking a glass with them.
- The host shouldn't say a toast thanking everyone unless it's time to leave.
- The best things about toasts—they are an excellent opportunity to air grievances / send not-so-subtle messages to your loved ones. Basically its a low key roast, and our family's toasts include things like "next year may you be kinder," "I'm looking forward to grandchildren," let's toast to "future moms' ' on March 8th/Mother's Day.

Three cultures for the price of one

Connecting with my identity as Russian or Ukrainian was a given considering where I was born, American culture was the one I adopted upon immigrating, and Jewish culture was the last piece of self-exploration that I didn't even know I needed. One fun way to explore all of the cultures was to celebrate holidays!

May day celebration – author atop dad's shoulders, mom, aunt

A BIRD'S EYE CALENDAR VIEW OF SOME HOLIDAYS MY FAMILY MIGHT HAVE CELEBRATED IN THE MID 90'S (WHEN WE FIRST IMMIGRATED)

WINTER

December 8 [SOVIET] The day Stalin's constitution was ratified

---

December 25 [AMERICAN] Christmas also known as Jews eat at Chinese restaurants day

---

December 31 [SOVIET] Non-ideological holiday state-sanctioned celebration of the New Year

---

January 1 [GLOBAL] New Year's Day

January 7 [RUSSIAN ORTHODOX] Рождество [Rozhdestvo], a Russian Orthodox holiday celebrating the birth of Christ

---

January 14 (Two weeks after New Year's) [SOVIET] Старый Новый год [Staryy Novyy god] Old New Year

---

February 2 [SOVIET] Масленица [Maslenitsa] Leftover from Pagan rituals, Day of the Sun. The Russian Orthodox church adopted this holiday and called it Maslenitsa, celebrated by making crepes to represent the sun. After this there was a 42-day lent (no meat, no white bread, no animal products)

February 14 [AMERICAN] Valentines Day

February 23 [SOVIET] День защи́тника Оте́чества [den zaschetnika otchestva] Defender of the Fatherland Day was celebrated for the achievement of military and veterans, but has essentially evolved into Men's Day.

SPRING

March 8 [SOVIET/GLOBAL] International Women's Day

April (typically in April as this is tracked via a lunar calendar) [RUSSIAN ORTHODOX] Пасха [paskha] Easter The dome-shaped baked goods made on this day represent the dome of a church.

April 12 [SOVIET] Kosmonaut Day. Unofficial holiday celebrating the accomplishment of the Soviet Space Program. On this day in 1961, Yuri Gagarin became the first human being to fly into space.

April 22 [SOVIET] Lenin's Birthday (not a red calendar day).

May 1 [SOVIET/GLOBAL] International Day of Labor.

May 9 [SOVIET] Day of victory over Nazis. Set up by Kruschev. Also a memorial day for those that lost their lives.

SUMMER

June 1 [SOVIET/GLOBAL] International Children's Day.

August 28 [SOVIET] Day of the Navy.

FALL

September 1 [SOVIET] First day of school, Day of Knowledge.

November 7 [SOVIET] Celebrating the October Revolution (due to the calendar change, it's in November).

November 4th Thursday [AMERICAN] Thanksgiving

Bonus Soviet Holidays:

There were also holidays to celebrate each labor sect such as March 23, Day of Theater or May 28, Day of Border Patrol.

Bonus Russian Orthodox holidays:

Saints Day, Tsarist Russia. You would frequently name a child based on their saints day (except for the less popular saints).

A VERY UN AMERICAN THANKSGIVING, MY FAVORITE HOLIDAY

> This is a **HOHMA** - a joke or a funny, witty tale

What I love about being Russian, Jewish, and growing up in America is that my family celebrated every. single. holiday.

International Women's Day? Buy flowers, pamper the ladies, and throw a feast!

Hanukkah? Peek inside a synagogue and ready yourself for eight days of merriment!

Flag Day? Hoist 'em up and drink 'til you see stars and stripes!

As a kid, I thought all this celebrating was because my parents were eager to embrace our new country by immersing themselves in American culture while remaining mindful of our Russian roots and Jewish traditions.

Now that I'm a little older and wiser, I realize they just like to party.

When we first adopted the American holidays, including Thanksgiving, my parents would invite friends and family over, cook a huge Russian feast (a minimum of seventeen dishes), and observe the one all-important tradition—plenty of ice-cold Vodka.

Despite my begging, pleading, and incessant screenings of *A Charlie Brown Thanksgiving* for what an authentic Thanksgiving meal should look like, no consideration was given to the "American food" typically served for this holiday. I'm pretty sure the only reason we even had a turkey was because it was on sale. (I grew to be resentful of turkey because for weeks after Thanksgiving my parents would procure a turkey from their overstuffed freezer and make it for dinner. And lunch. And breakfast.)

As for the trimmings? We served completely unAmerican things like fur coat (a dish made by layering pickled herring, onions, beets, and lots of mayonnaise); my grandmother's infamous egg, cheese, and garlic salad; blintzes with sour cream and caviar, and on and on and on, with plenty of dill on top.

Then as the years went by, the "American" turkey was joined by a sprinkling of traditional Thanksgiving fares like green beans or a solitary sweet potato. By the mid-90s our table began to resemble a Las Vegas-style buffet dinner with its hodgepodge of culinary concoctions.

It bordered on the ridiculous.

The poor cooks in charge of this holiday meal began to grumble... "We'll never eat all of this" or "Herring and turkey really don't go together..." And while they were met with resistance at first, "It's just not a proper feast without Gefilte fish!" Slowly but surely, one dill-topped-dish at a time was being phased out.

And then the first child in our family, my cousin, was born in America. She was a real American. She could even run for President, or Miss America! That's the year my aunt (her mother) bought a Martha Stewart cookbook and took over the Thanksgiving meal. She did it all – the turkey, the yams, two kinds of cranberry sauce, and even a homemade pecan pie.

We've had my Aunt's Thanksgiving Dinner for nine years running now. We won't let her change a thing on the menu. It's all TRADITION now.

Thanksgiving is my favorite holiday for many reasons, the meal being the highest on the list. And while I am so grateful for this country and my family, and blah blah blah something else sentimental, my only Thanksgiving wish is that my aunt would make stuffing this year. But apparently, some things are still just too American.

*BREAKING NEWS

my aunt made stuffing in 2021, this is it people we are officially full on Amerikantsi now

Gefilte Fish

Ingredients

4-5 trout
1 onion
5-6 eggs
3-4 tbsp matza meal

Instructions

- Carefully remove skin of the fish and set aside for stuffing.
 Clean trout by removing bones and head, set bones and head aside.
- Food process fish together with a slightly browned onion.
- Add 1 tsp salt, sugar, vegetable oil.
- Separate egg whites and beat into soft peaks, add yellows to it and mix some more.
- Add eggs to fish.
- Add matza meal to fish.
- Knead like dough with your hands.
- Taste test to make sure there's enough salt, sugar.
- Use an oval pot to accommodate the fish if possible, cut carrot, beets, onion, onion skin, all the bones, add a grate/trivet.
- Start with a layer of fish skin and add mixture to it, add skin on top, roll with parchment paper and tie the ends of the paper together, make any leftover into a fishball.
- Put in pot, place pieces of carrot/beets between the fish so paper doesn't stick together, pour boiling water in the corner of the pot and it gradually fills the pot with water.
- Bring to a boil, reduce heat and let simmer 1-2 hours.
- Cut the ends and carefully remove from paper.

American Holidays Soviet-style

The truly beautiful thing about our journey in this country is that as the years go by, our dinner table becomes a true melting pot. Over time we've lovingly incorporated traditions and customs into our lives. Our New Year's celebrations now include a nod to the upcoming Lunar New Year with my grandmother handing out small toys or ornaments to commemorate the animal of the Lunar New Year and our menus are frequently inspired by the myriad cuisines and cultures that we experience in America. This was especially the case after my dad spent several years owning and operating a Taqueria—a Mexican food restaurant—and learned to roll burritos, cook Menudo, and make Salvadorian pupusas with the best of them!

Here's one recipe that's evolved thanks to living in America... a

Super American!

Солёная рыба
Salted Salmon

Ingredients

2lbs of sushi grade* atlantic salmon filet, preferably middle cut (not near the head or tail)
salt
sugar

Instructions

- Remove skin and any remaining bones from salmon filet, wash and pat dry.
- Lay salmon on foil and add 1 level Tbsp of salt per pound and 1 tsp of sugar per pound.
- Massage salt and sugar into the filet.
- Cover with foil.
- Put in the refrigerator for at least six hours.
- Remove from the refrigerator, wash and dry.
- Get a new sheet of foil and add olive oil (or garlic infused olive oil.)
- Add salmon, add some more olive oil and rub it in.
- Cover with foil and place in the refrigerator for at least twenty minutes.
- Cut and serve.

My Dad's recipe is somewhere in between traditional cured salmon and sashimi because it uses less salt and is not cured as long as other cured fish recipes. Use sushi grade salmon or consume at your own risk.

RELIGION AND THEOLOGY IN THE USSR

Ah yes religion in the Soviet Union - quite the paradox. On the one hand, the state was officially atheist and atheism was touted as a core value of the socialist system. On the other hand, in the Soviet Union many people continued to practice a variety of religious traditions in private. And on the other other hand, no matter what secret religion you were or weren't, you better not be Jewish. So it was particularly tricky when my Ukrainian dad did the unthinkable and married a Jewish woman. This ~~devastated~~ concerned my dad's parents greatly, and a secret plan was put into motion to save my soul and have me baptized.

From left to right: Shura, mom Marina, Aleksi

HOLY WATER

I stood motionless for a brief moment while my mom unclasped the small gold cross from *my neck.*

"*We're going to put this away, and you can't tell anyone about it.*"

I put my weight on my right foot... then my left.

"*This is a secret. A secret between you and God. God will only protect you if you don't tell. Understand?*"

My olive-colored soldiers were about to fight a great battle, and they needed me to lead them! I shrugged my shoulders. And with that enthusiastic and wordless solemn vow, I was dismissed.

I couldn't understand why my mom was so upset when I came home from my summer with grandma Sasha wearing my new cross. I didn't understand a lot of things that happened that summer.

I had so many adventures; collisions with bikes, boys, and birch trees. I had earned each scrape and bruise, bloodied toenail, and bee-sting. It was a miracle there weren't broken bones. But grandma didn't see the miracles, she only saw that because of who my mother was, I didn't have an angel watching over me, and she set about to fix that.

She made me wear a dress with a high collar that itched and itched. We walked to the church purposefully, but I dragged my feet, and the dust swirled about, ruining my crisp new tights. Grandma tried to explain it to me again, the water would be like dying and being born again, but it didn't make any sense.

The priest wore a tall hat and circled around me. The women peered at me, squinting their eyes in judgment and whispered behind my back. "*She's so old*" "*Why didn't they do this earlier?*"

The priest poured water on my head without warning, and I clasped my hands to my chest to stop the trickle making its way down my body. The circle of people around me contracted and began to chant. Terrified, I cried and clung to my grandma.

Then it was over. I was Baptized.

I wasn't really sure what that meant. I wasn't sure what it meant when my grandma, my dad's mom, emphasized that I was, first and foremost, a Ukrainian girl, either. But I wore my cross for the rest of the summer. It made my grandma happy, and that was a small miracle in itself.

As I grew up, I began to understand more (or less.) Kids were calling me names and my mom's and my passport was stamped "Jewess." I wasn't a Ukrainian girl, and no amount of Holy Water was going to change that.

MY EMERGING JEWISH IDENTITY, A TIMELINE:

So how did a secretly baptized, Jewish girl, evolve her understanding of her Jewish identity? Well I present to you a timeline of my emerging Jewish identity:

Step one: finding out

I've been confused about Jewishness and Judaism practically since preschool. You would be too if this happened to you. A preschool classmate called me a "zhydovka." When I ask my parents what this is, I find out three things. One, that "zhydovka" is a racial slur for a Jewish woman. Two, that (great news!) **I am** a Jewish woman. And three, our country has a long history of anti-semitism (not liking Jewish people, to put it mildly.) Finding out I'm Jewish is particularly confusing news as I am four years old and obviously I already have a firm belief system that has nothing to do with a formal religious identity. (I later find out that my beliefs most closely resemble animism—the attribution of a soul to plants, inanimate objects, and natural phenomena.)

Step two: confusion aka my secret baptism

My dad's mom, who was already less than thrilled that my dad had knocked up a Jewess (see above antisemitism), is legitimately concerned for my soul when one summer I have not one, but two major bike accidents back-to-back. She decides, for the safety of my soul, to baptize me into Russian Orthodoxy. This is a secret twice over. One, because of communism and the government ban on religion of any kind, and two, because even though there's no religion, I thought I was supposed to be Jewish. *Isn't that what my classmate accused me of?*

Step three: exploration

After we immigrate to America, we are offered a free year of tuition at Hebrew Academy through the endless generosity of Jewish Family and Children's Services. I visit and find out that Hebrew school means wearing long skirts. Hard pass.

In middle school, I begin to attend - Youth Alive, Christian after school programming that I don't even realize is religious in nature. Even after I connect the dots about this Jesus person they keep talking about I continue attending because: free food.

In high school, my best friend Stella and I strike out to embrace Judaism and attend high holidays services at the local Chabad house. She's shamed for wearing a low-cut shirt and told to cover up. We never go back.

In college, friends visiting me at UC Davis convince me to go check out the Jewish interest sorority rush because MTV is filming it. I turn down my chance at stardom by not living in the "pledge house" supplied by production (to tape our every move) but I do experience my first meaningful connections to Judaism and Jewishness through this unexpected sisterhood: the Sigma Alpha Epsilon Pi sorority. Singing Lech Lecha, standing in the Havdalah circle and being surrounded by incredible Jewish (and non-Jewish) women, who are living by an ancient set of values that speak deeply to me.

My final year at UC Davis, I'm the program coordinator for the UC Davis Hillel House, a Jewish organization on college campuses. I don't know how I ended up getting this job being as clueless about Judaism as I was, but here I start to get a sense of some of the rules and practices of Judaism: kashrut, prayers, holidays. One particular Hillel House attendee makes it his job to follow me around to ensure I kept strict kosher by using separate dishes and cutlery for the meat and dairy. It's more than a little overwhelming.

Step four: adrift

Without a post-college tether to Jewishness I'm floating off into space again until it's time for my wedding. My equally Jew-ish husband-to-be and I debate how theoretically Jewish our wedding will actually be and which Jewish traditions we might actually include. We do things to appease our families or because our wedding is theater themed and so this feels like another piece of the performance. But also, on some level I am connected; I feel an inexplicable attraction to these traditions, perhaps anticipating that a moment may come in the future where this wedding will become the Jewish foundation we can build our lives on. The ketubah (or marriage contract), in particular, is quite meaningful for us, and once we (finally) find our perfect egalitarian modern ketubah, we divide up its text and speak its words as our wedding vows. (Fun fact, we accidentally served our Rabbi tref—non-kosher food, in this case smoked eel—at our wedding banquet. Oops!)

When I am pregnant with my first daughter, I experience a brief return to formal religious practice. She is breech, and in my desperation to have a natural birth, I attempt everything to get this baby to turn, including attending Shabbat services at synagogue. This is a bit like suddenly turning to prayer on the eve of a big school exam and so it doesn't exactly stick.

Step five: acceptance

As I get older, I take on the emceeing duties of every Jewish holiday we celebrate. I relish my role as amateur Jewish educator and homegrown cantor. I even take on Passover Seder, though truth be told this is still above and beyond my capabilities, I can't even name all the plagues!

However, as my firstborn gets older and approaches the age of maturity (from a Jewish perspective), I insist on her studying and having a bat mitzvah ceremony. This is an easier sell once I also explain about the bat mitzvah party she'll get to have. I figure if she's going to reject who she is one day, she can at least have a clearer sense of what she's rejecting.

On the day of her bat mitzvah, in Sherith Israel, arguably the most beautiful synagogue in the world, my daughter confidently recites her Torah portion in front of friends and family. Her great-grandmother—my grandmother Baba Liliya, who was born on the day Nazis invaded our country—responds to my daughter's prayers in Hebrew, a distant linguistic cousin of the Yiddish Liliya heard her own parents speaking in childhood. During this call and response between my grandmother and my daughter, some of the confusion inside of me settles into place. My frequent questions of *Who am I and how do I fit into this world?* have a new answer. I am many things: Soviet-born, storyteller, speaker, but in this moment, I am also the torch bearer passing down pieces of our past to the next generation. And my fire blazes bright with pride.

Rabbi Jessica Graf, Baba Liliya, daughter, Cantor Toby Glaser

I WAS BROUGHT TO THIS COUNTRY TO MAKE MY MOTHER CRY.

I come to America, fresh-faced young girl. My belly is empty (is added for dramatic effect), but my heart is full of hope, deworming medication, and dreams.

Like many immigrants who are employed in their home country as doctor or engineer but whose credentials are overlooked in America, I too am facing harsh reality of compulsory schooling placement test.

Result?

I am eight years old and already a bitter disappointment, as according to a test I am "average eight-year-old." and recommended to begin second grade. Parents cry and tell me they did not bring me to this country to have me fail. (This, we call foreshadowing.)

I gain mastery of English language, "McDonalds, Reagonomics, Beam me up Scotty!" I am still on average trajectory and do not skip grades. Parents are inconsolable. But I apply myself to the arts, following in their path, in our home country parents were distinguished stage directors.

In fifth grade, I land lead in school play. Success! Parents see performance on opening night and cry. They tell me play was produced completely unprofessional, as if by children, and they did not bring me to this country to have me fail.

I am accepted to college. Parents momentarily overcome with joy! I explain this College is not Harvard, Yale, or Stanford. Parents cry.

During high school graduation, I am awarded prize for community service to school. Parents cry and tell me they did not bring me to this country to have me become social worker. They refuse all pictures for memory preserving of "shameful pseudo communist award."

In college, I select "Communications" as major. Parents think I'm making joke. When they see it on my diploma, they cry and tell me to go back to college and finish with a degree this time, they did not bring me to this country so that I would refuse respectable career path of Doctor, Lawyer, Engineer, or in the case of woman: Accountant.

I meet the love of my life. He is Russian and Jewish. Success! Parents momentarily overcome with joy and relief! I announce that love of my life is moving us to Reno. My parents cry and tell me they did not bring me to this country to achieve oxymoronic accomplishment of living in the Biggest Little City (in sin!).

I give birth to a daughter, and I make my mother Babushka.

Together we cry.

*Author at 1 years old
Typical Soviet photo studio*

Author 5 years old

EVERYDAY CELEBRATIONS

Unlike an American parents' approach of celebrating a noteworthy accomplishment, a good report card for instance, with a special meal, my parent's approach is - there is no reason to hold a special celebration if every meal is special - and so they have always treated every meal time as a special occasion.

What this means, practically speaking, is that my parents take great care to elevate the eating experience by:

- serving первое, второе, третье* even if it's not an elaborate banquet and just a casual dinner at their house they still manage to serve courses: appetizers, entree, and a dessert
- decorating a dish украшают [ukrashayut] with herbs or radish/carrot flowers
- taking leftovers and zhuzhing them up освежают [osvezhayut] or "refreshing" them with a new ingredient
- setting the table with proper dinnerware and utensils
- making sure to turn on the lights, so that it's a festive environment

> *DEFINITION
> 'первое, второе, третье'
> means first, second, third

I've learned a lot from my parents–I can turn leftovers into something amazing (this is especially applicable to restaurant leftovers) and I am all about presentation and can make a stunning plate (you should see my insane grazing tables and charcuterie boards). However, I am less skilled at the brass tacks of cooking and I can't even comprehend baking. A friend recently texted asking to borrow a cake pan and my unironic response was 'what is a cake pan?'

All this to say, the person that needs these everyday celebrations most is me.

Depending on your perspective, In the Soviet Union, there were either no reasons to celebrate anything or there was a daily opportunity to give thanks for surviving yet another day.

Some simple reasons to celebrate were...

Successfully tricking and subverting the Soviet government! Anytime you could get one over on the authorities was a reason to celebrate! For example, the way to sneak banned Western music was to burn a cassette tape and then painstakingly re-package them up to look like they were new and unopened. One of my dad's most epic subversions was how he got all of their diplomas out of the country. He put them right in the suitcase matching the color of the diploma to the color of the clothes, proving that the best way to hide something is always in plain sight.

Something else to celebrate was acquiring... anything! A pair of jeans or a new pair of shoes was always exciting. In an oppressive regime, there was a rich artistic tradition. So much art was created and consumed, especially satire and humor so books and art were coveted as well.

FAQ PART TWO

And now it's time for some less frequently asked questions...

Q: Who did your family live with in the Soviet Union? Was your apartment big?
   A: *Twelve of us lived in one apartment.*
   All 78 square meters (not including the bathroom) housed my mom Marina, my dad Peter and myself, my mom's younger sister Natasha, her mom Liliya, dad Vladimer, my mom's dad's mom (the Ukrainian) Musya and (Jewish) dad Abram (scandalous!) and dad's younger sister Tatyana, her husband—also Vladimer—and their two kids Sasha and Sergei. Here is the layout of the apartment, which was typical of Soviet dwellings:

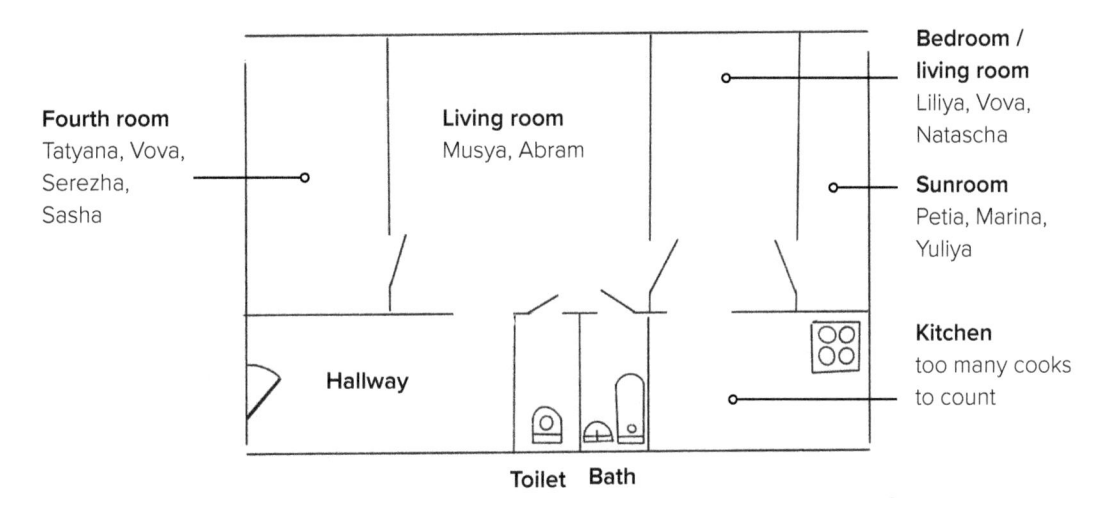

Fourth room
Tatyana, Vova, Serezha, Sasha

Living room
Musya, Abram

Bedroom / living room
Liliya, Vova, Natascha

Sunroom
Petia, Marina, Yuliya

Kitchen
too many cooks to count

Hallway

Toilet **Bath**

There were, simply put, too many cooks in that kitchen!

Q: Is it true everyone lived with strangers in the Soviet Union?
   A: *Sort of. Soviet authorities in Stalin's time considered private kitchens, dining rooms, and even apartments to be*

> ***FUN FACT**
> *One bathroom - 12 people. Particularly fun during shortages on toilet paper.*

111

dangerous to the regime. This combined with the lack of available housing meant that multiple families were often assigned to live together, sometimes blood relatives and other times complete strangers. People would have their own bedrooms but have to share bathrooms and kitchens - known as a communal kitchens or коммуналка [komunnalka] often with just one fridge and one stove for multiple families.

Q: At least you got to live with family members and not a bunch of randos, that was easier right?

A: We were lucky to share our kitchen with just blood relatives but still it was a complicated ballet. Musya cooked for the whole family, but as the family grew, each matriarch began to cook for her own family. It worked well until one day, as family lore tells us, my dad ate all the колбаса [kolbasa] cold cuts. After that Musya cooked for her and Tanya's family, Liliya cooked for her family, and my dad began to cook for ours. Dad was a self-taught chef and worked in high-end restaurants in Moscow as a teen. He had seen things the rest of us could only dream of- he'd even tried bear!

Q: Did you always eat at home or were there other options?

A: I'm so glad you asked, here I made you a little chart of eating options outside the home:

> *FUN FACT
>
> *Bread and mustard were free, but you were discouraged from taking more bread than you needed. There were signs like* **хлеб драгоценность, им не сори** *[hleb dragozenost, im ne soree] bread is precious, do not waste it*

- Столовая **[Stolovaya] Canteen** - in a canteen* you would take a tray and serve yourself pre-plated закуски [zakuski] appetizers, next an old mean lady would make you choose between the two soups [pervoye], then a different mean lady would prompt you to select the entree, finally the компот [kompot] fruit compote was self service
- Кафетерия **[Kafeteriya] Cafeteria** - served a limited menu of coffee, milk cocktail, cake or baked good
- Кулинария **[Kulinariya]** - offered partially prepared food (also known as полуфабрикат [polu fabrikat], it was a lot like many of the options at a Trader Joes for example

- Бистро **[Bistro] Cafe** - this was like a canteen but someone will serve you, the food was simpler and less expensive than a restaurant, according to my dad this is named after the word "quickly" in Russian - быстро [bistro]
- Ресторан **[Restoran] Restaurant** - full service restaurant, but at lunch there was usually a prefixed menu
- Домовая кухня **[Domovaya kuhnya] Home kitchen** - during lunch time (12-2) you would typically go home to eat, but if you lived too far from work you could visit one of these, which was similar to a canteen but had food на вынос [na vinos] to go.
- **Specialty stores or stands** that sell just one thing like пельменная [pel'mennaya], пирожковая [pirozhkovaya] which served pirozhki and broth, as well stands that sold kvas, beer, or ice cream

Q: Did people eat three meals a day?

A: Here's a breakdown of when people usually ate their meals and the type of food they might enjoy

- 7am завтрак [zavtrak] breakfast: porridge made of farina, buckwheat, rice, cold cuts cheese, bread, tea
- 11am optional второй завтрак [vtoroy zavtrak] second breakfast which translates to mid-day: snacks like an apple, a slice of bread
- 1-2pm обед [obed] essentially lunch: always started first course - soup, second course which had an animal protein with a side dish, topped off with third course - a small dessert or a sweet drink
- 4pm полудник [poludnik] optional snack served in nursery schools and the like, usually something like milk and cookies
- 6-7pm ужин [uzhin] supper: this could be a smaller second course, I remember eating buckwheat with eggs or sausage for example, or it could be a baked good with tea, some people would have a glass of kefir an hour before bed as it was said to improve digestion

Of course there were foods that you could eat at any time of day like, Сырники [Sirniki]...

Yelena's Sneaky Сырники Sirniki

Makes 25 Sirniki, enough for Grandma to feed two children and have enough leftover for Mom and Dad so no one gets mad

Ingredients

2 granny smith apples
2 medium zucchini
1lb farmers cheese or cottage cheese
flour *(amount and type depends on the type of cheese you are using, if using cottage cheese you can use farina, if using farmers cheese, start with ½ a cup of flour and add as needed)*
2 eggs
½ tsp baking soda
½ tsp salt
1 tsp vanilla
1-2 tbsp sugar (optional)

Optional: *raisins, other dried fruit*
Vegetable oil and butter for frying

Instructions

- Finely grate apples and zucchini, squeeze out the juice.
- Combine apples and zucchini with farmers cheese, eggs, baking soda, salt, vanilla, sugar, and any optional dried fruit like raisins.
- Gradually mix in flour until the batter resembles wet dough.
- Use a spoon to scoop the batter directly onto a hot pan greased with vegetable oil and a bit of butter, fry on both sides.

Serve with jam, sour cream, honey or your favorite sweet toppings.

Q: Is it true that there were no cookbooks in Russia?
A: *Untrue! There was one. And why would anyone need more?*
The one official cookbook - Книга о вкусной и здоровой пище [Kniga o vkusnoi i zdorovoi pishche] "The book of tasty and healthy food" first published in the 1930s received updated editions throughout the Soviet Union time period and was thought of as the culinary bible.

Q: Did people diet?
A: *Here's some Soviet style dieting advice as (supplied by mother in law)*

If you want to go on a diet here's an excellent diet to try!
In the morning have секс (sex)
In the afternoon have кекс keks (cake),
And in the evening have секс
If the diet isn't working, cut out the кекс .

Q: Speaking of sex, is it true there was no birth control in the Soviet Union?
A: *Put it to you this way, I've heard many jokes that children are "the abortions my doctor refused to perform."*

Q: Was it difficult raising kids?
A: *It's as difficult as it was anywhere. Raising little kids is tough, but again my mother-in-law supplies these words to live by:*
Маленькие детки маленькие бедки подрастают детки подрастают бедки
[Malen'kiye detki malen'kiye bedki podrastayut detki podrastayut bedki]
The literal translation is small kids = small problems, and bigger kids = bigger problems. We know this in America as 'mo money mo problems'.
But one of the benefits of living intergenerationally was that child care was much more readily available. My parents both worked full time during odd hours (theater people, ya know?) and were supported by willing and not so willing caregivers. My mom's paternal grandmother (Babushka Muysa) took care of me most days because she was the only one not working outside the home by then. My aunt (who was twelve when I was born) got other fun duties like cleaning the doodies off of the diapers (everyone cloth-dia-

pered, it was so chic! they had no choice.)

Q: What was growing up as a child like in the soviet union?

A: In theory you were in training to be a good citizen of the Soviet state, which included doing well in school, keeping very neat and tidy, and having an official rank in the communist party starting in 2nd grade!

My childhood however was also full of whimsy, creativity and exploration, particularly in the summer when I would visit my paternal grandparents.....

Preschool celebration

116

MINI BITES FROM THE GARDEN

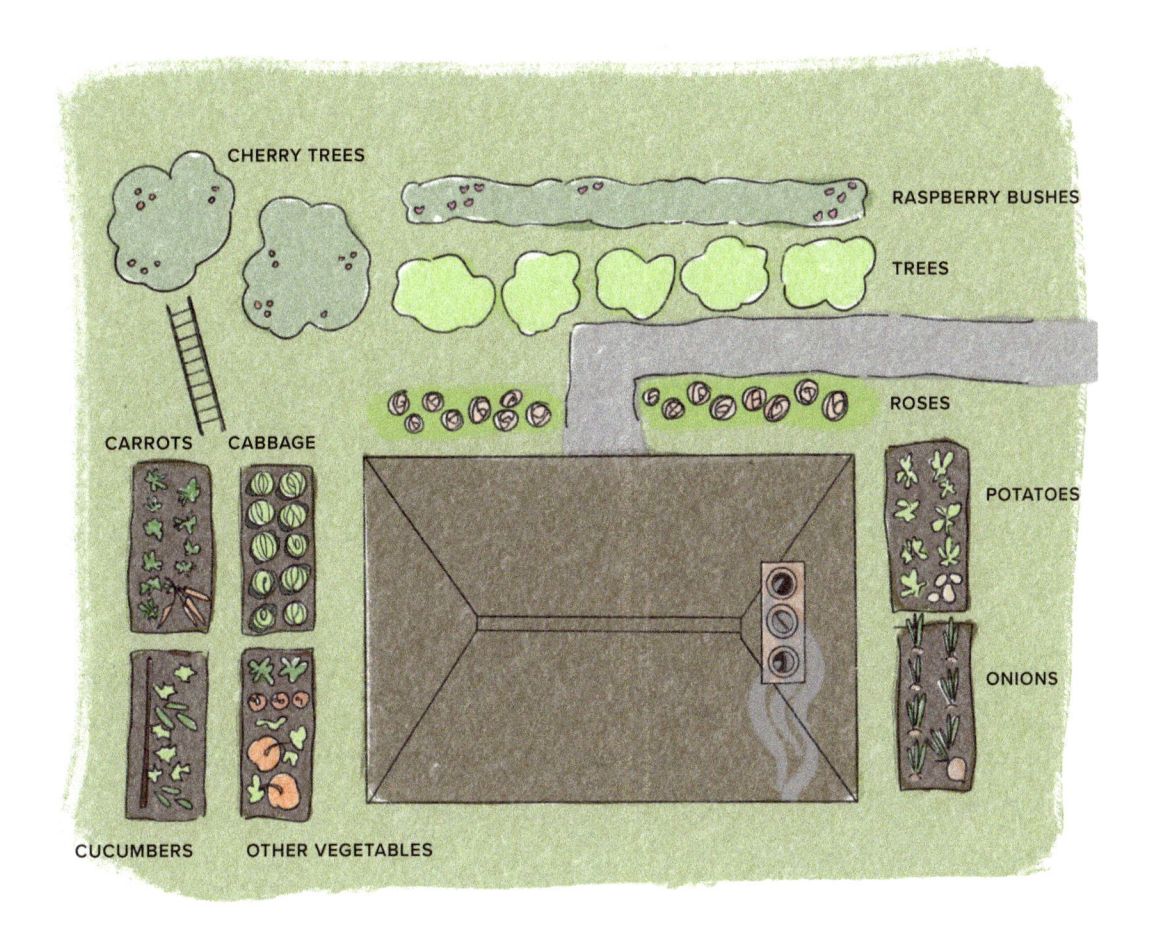

- **Rabbits.** We had a rabbit pen where we kept anywhere from eight to ten rabbits. I always loved taking care of them in the summertime, feeding them and brushing their fur. But during an off-season visit in winter, I discovered the harsh truth: the key ingredient in grandma's rabbit stew was (spoiler alert) rabbit.

- **Chickens and Eggs.** We had a chicken coop, and one of my chores was to collect eggs in the morning. I remember that the eggs were usually still warm, and occasionally my grandma would poke a hole at the top of one and I would just drink it raw.
- **Cherry Tree.** The tree that inadvertently injured me. I would often climb this tree and gather cherries from the bottom branches but for the cherries at the very top we would use a ladder. One day, I climbed to the top of the ladder and fell backwards – cartoon style. Turns out the ladder wasn't attached at the top, *d'oh*!
- **Potato Bugs.** One of my many chores was to collect the potato bugs off of the potatoes and place them in a glass jar. This was tedious work perfectly suited to a small child's hands!
- **Raspberry Bushes.** The bushes that comforted me in my time of need. One day, my grandfather, a carpenter by trade, and a metalsmith by hobby, was tinkering around and cutting metal rods. I eagerly volunteered to help him, and without any protective gear or common sense, he let me! Next thing you know, a small piece of metal flew off the torch and lodged itself above my right eye. In shock I sprinted across the garden and huddled up in the raspberry bushes for comfort. The piece of metal shows up in my x-rays to this day.
- **Not So Easy Bake Oven.** One afternoon I decided to make an outdoor oven. I went around the neighborhood borrowing (read: stealing) supplies – bricks, makeshift mortar, and tools. Then I put it together! My grandparents let me try baking potatoes in it. I learned a valuable lesson that day: ovens have holes for the smoke to exit.
- **Santa Squirrel.** Ever so often I would wake up to find that a squirrel had left nuts for me on my window sill. This squirrel may or may not have been my grandfather.
- **Kitchen connections.** When I wasn't climbing trees or challenging the neighborhood boys to (barefoot!) foot races. I spent a lot of time in the kitchen with my grandma.Togehrer we made pelmeni, canned tomatoes, shelled peas, and prepared cherries for jam.

If you liked these mini food stories from my grandparents garden,
I hope you enjoy one that's not so mini:

TEARS OF MY TREE

> **TSURIS** *this story is about hard or difficult times*

I snuck a fistful of nails in my pocket, took my tiny hammer and skipped off to practice what he had taught me.

Hold the nail in one hand, the hammer in the other, up high by the neck. Steady your hand on the wood and give it a few short smacks until the tip of the nail is wedged in. Swing cautiously but confidently, give it a few solid whacks until the job is done.

I had practiced on the cast-off pieces of wood in my grandpa's make-shift carpentry shop, on the shelves in the garage, on the fence to our yard. But there was a whole forest of timber in the garden that I had yet to practice on.

Like Goldilocks, I considered the possibilities.

Seedlings? Too thin. Shrubs? Too bushy. My favorite cherry tree? Tall, strong, with a bark too thick and flaky, too hard to penetrate.

But the walnut tree I could wrap my hands around twice! Not too thin, not too thick.

It seemed a perfect choice.

Holding the nail steady, I twisted into the trunk and scraped below the surface. The outer layer was paper-thin and green underneath. One quick smack and another.

I couldn't wiggle the nail in any direction, it was firmly embedded in the trunk now. I stood back, satisfied with a job well done, smile on my face, hip cocked to the side.

An amber-colored liquid began to trickle out.

This was no lifeless hunk of wood or willing garage shelf. This was a living thing!

It sighed deeply, the tears continued to pour down its body, and I began to comprehend the horror of what I had done.

I leaned in, touched my forehead to the wetness, whispered, "I'm sorry," and ran to find my grandfather. I led him to my tree and showed him the injury.

I considered and rejected an elaborate tale of nail-wielding bandits and instead, confessed, without a lot of fanfare. He said he admired my honesty and would take that into account when doling out punishment.

He need not have bothered with any such thing.

As the tears continued to flow from the tree, so did mine. I sobbed and begged for forgiveness. What possessed me to do this wicked thing? I reassured my tree that I didn't mean it, that whatever demon guided my hand was gone, and I would never let the tree come to harm again. I covered the injury with old t-shirts and pleaded with my grandparents to let me sleep next to the tree that night. They allowed it, but must have moved me at nightfall.

I awoke to find the amber crusted over the hole and the tree looking sturdy and as strong as ever.

It has forgiven you, my grandpa reassured me. But had I forgiven myself?

THE FOOD IN/OUT LIST

Foods I hated as a child:

Cooked cabbage

Борщ Borscht (because of the aforementioned cabbage)

Голубцы Golubtsi (wrapped in cabbage! gah)

Prunes

Foods I loved as a child:

Buckwheat with eggs

Вафельный торт [vaffelniy tort] waffle cake

Grated apple and carrot salad in daycare

Пирожки [piroshki]

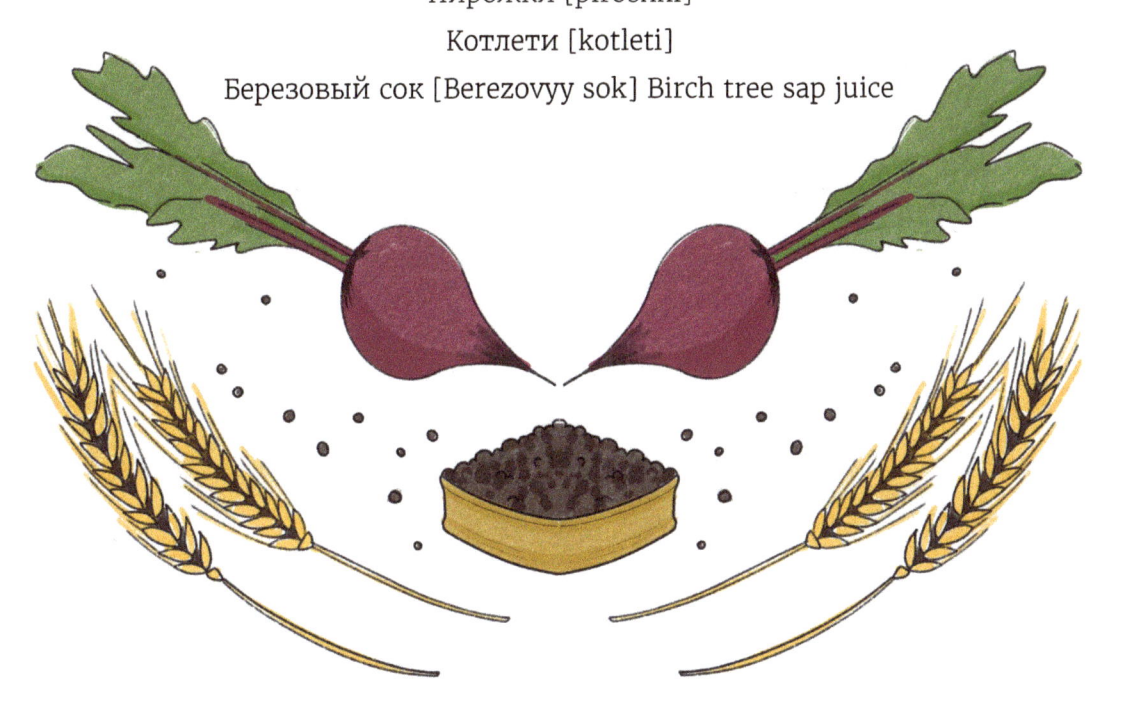

Котлети [kotleti]

Березовый сок [Berezovyy sok] Birch tree sap juice

Борщ
Borscht

Ingredients

2 lb beef shank with bone
2 medium yellow onions
3 medium carrots
2 small beets or 1 medium to large
½ can tomato paste (or fresh tomatoes if in season)
1 bay leaf
2 medium stalks celery
parsley root if available
½ medium green cabbage or 1 small
4-5 medium potatoes
Salt to taste
If you have stems from parsley, mint, or basil you can add those to your herb bouquet

Instructions

- Start by making broth: wash beef shanks, place beef shanks in a pot and cover a pot ¾ with water, let it boil and remove the film, set to a gentle simmer.
- Take celery, one carrot, bay leaf, any additional herb stems and wrap with kitchen twine, add to simmering water.
- Remove one onion skin but do not chop the onion and add to simmering water.
- Add one Tbsp of salt, cover and let simmer for an hour to hour and a half, the meat should be separating from the bone but not falling apart.
- Chop cabbage finely and place in cold water.
- Cube remaining onion, grate two carrots, peel beets and set aside.
- Peel potatoes and chop into medium cubes, put in water.
- Once the meat is cooked remove everything from the pot, cube the meat, keep the carrot and compost the rest.
- Add beets to the broth and bring to a boil.
- Once it boils, allow it to gently simmer for 20-25 minutes until you can poke through the beet.
- Fry onions in a pan with vegetable oil (corn, sunflower, blend) until onions are translucent, add carrots to the pan and mix together, add cubed shanks and fry everything until carrots are soft, add boiled carrot from the broth to this and just mash with a fork.
- Remove beets from broth and set aside to cool.

- Allow the broth to boil again.
- Add potatoes and reduce heat slightly to bring to a boil again.
- Once it begins boiling, reduce heat and add a half can of tomato paste.
- Cover and allow gentle boil until potatoes are almost cooked.
- Grate the beets.
- Add grated beets to the pan with onion and carrots, mix well, and then turn off the heat. Drain cabbage and add to the broth.
- After five minutes or so, add your fried onion, carrot, and beet mix to the soup.
- Increase the heat and allow everything to mix together until cabbage is cooked but not overcooked.
- Taste, and if needed, add a few Tbsp of ketchup for a sweet and sour flavor.
- Ready to serve, but best on the second day.

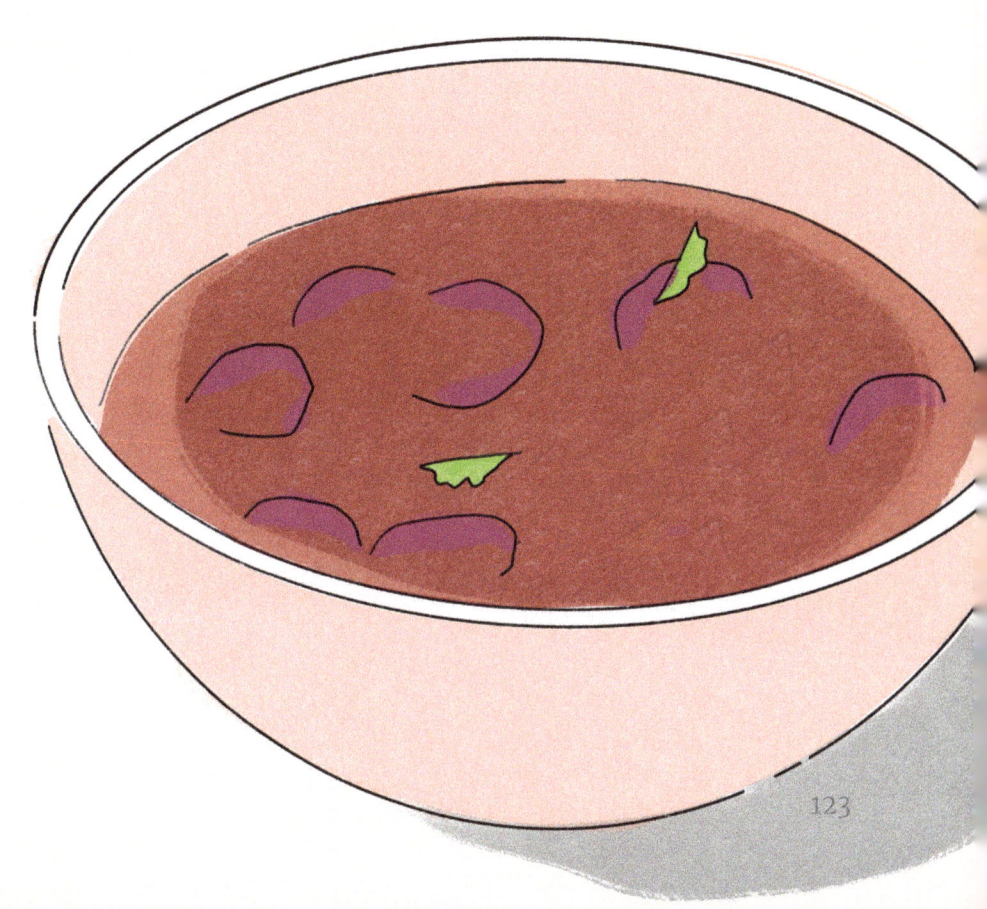

Капустняк или Щи
Kapustnyak or Schii

Ingredients

2 lb beef shank with bone
½ medium cabbage
3-4 potatoes
2 yellow onions *(1 bigger than the other)*
1 rib celery
2 medium carrots
¾ lb of pickled cabbage (homemade or store-bought)
4 tbsp corn or sunflower oil
30g butter
salt to taste *(keep in mind pickled cabbage is salty so don't overdo it)*
nutmeg to taste

Instructions

- Start by making the broth, wash beef shanks, and place beef shanks in a pot. Cover a pot ¾ with water, let it boil and remove the film.
- Add small peeled onion, one peeled carrot, and celery, and let it gently simmer until meat is falling off the bones, about 60-90 minutes.
- While the meat is cooking, prep your cabbage.
- Chiffonade the cabbage and submerge it in cold water.
- Cut the pickled cabbage to ensure uniform pieces and set aside.
- Fry onions in a pan with vegetable oil (corn, sunflower, or a blend) until onions are translucent, add carrots and mix together (you will add cubed shanks to this once cooked) and fry until carrots are soft, add boiled carrot from the broth and just mash with a fork.
- Once the meat is cooked, remove everything from the pot, cube the meat, keep the carrot, and compost the rest.
- Peel and cube potatoes and add to broth.
- Increase heat to bring to a boil again. Once boiled, reduce heat and let simmer for five minutes.
- Add pickled cabbage, let simmer for five to seven minutes.
- Remove cabbage from cold water and remove excess water.
- Add cabbage to broth and let simmer for five minutes.
- Add onion/carrot fried mix. Simmer a few more minutes, ensure that cabbage is al dente.
- Reduce heat and add butter.
- Add nutmeg (or a bit of vinegar).
- Turn off the heat, close the lid, and let it stand for fifteen minutes.
- Serve with sour cream!

Голубцы
Golubsti

Ingredients

2lb ground pork
1lb ground beef
4 carrots (1 small for the stuffing, 3 large for the sauce)
3 yellow onion (1 for the stuffing, 2 for the sauce)
1 clove garlic
1 egg
⅓ cups of arborio rice
2 tbsp chopped dill
6 oz. can of tomato paste
1 medium to large cabbage
3 tbsp corn oil
salt and pepper to taste

Instructions

- Remove the cabbage core with a knife so that later it's easier to take the cabbage apart. Get a large pot and fill it halfway with water, add salt and bring to a boil.
- Once boiling, add the head of cabbage with the hollow side down.
- Bring to a boil again, lower heat, and allow to simmer on medium to low heat for a few minutes.
- Flip the cabbage to hollow side up.
- Using two forks to gently begin to pull apart the cabbage leaves while the water continues to simmer.
- Put the cabbage leaves into a large mixing bowl.
- Once you reach the smallest leaves you can stop, it's difficult to fill these.
- While the cabbage cools you can make the sauce and filling.

For filling:

- Cook rice until almost al dente.
- Finely chop 1 onion and 1 clove of garlic.
- Grate 1 small carrot finely and combine with onion and garlic.
- Add dill to the mixture
- Once rice is cooked, rinse with cold water and add to the mixture.
- Add salt and pepper to taste.
- Mix everything thoroughly and set aside.

For sauce:

- Chop 2 onions into half circles.
- Grate 2 carrots.
- Dilute a whole can of tomato paste with 4 cups of water.
- In a large frying pan, fry chopped onions in corn oil (or any vegetable oil except olive) until golden.
- Add carrots to the pan and fry for two to three minutes.
- Add salt and pepper to taste.
- Add tomato water to the pan.
- Bring to a boil and let it simmer for a few minutes while the sauce thickens and then set aside.
- Once the cabbage leaves are cool, take one leaf at a time, remove the tip of the spine, the thickest part that is hard to bend, and set these trimmings aside.
- Cut very large leaves in half (removing the spine of these and setting the trimmings aside.)
- Try to sort the cabbage leaves by size and color.
- Get a large pot, dutch oven is ideal for this, and add all the cabbage trimmings to the bottom.
- Now it's time to fill the cabbage leaves!
- Depending on the size of the leaf, add filling and roll the leaf closed like a burrito. (Or you can try rolling the cabbage leaf like a roll and sticking the sides inside.)
- Add stuffed cabbage to the pot, larger pieces on the bottom and smaller pieces towards the top.
- Once finished, add sauce to the pan distributing evenly and making sure to cover your cabbage leaves, ensuring that all of the onion and carrot from the sauce is in the pot. Bring to a boil, then lower to low heat and let simmer for 45-50 min.

Пирожки
Pirozhki

There are many options for filling – savory cabbage with egg and green onion, potatoes with fried onion, mushroom, meat, organ meats, sweet: farmers cheese with dried fruit, sour cherry, apple, and more! We've included two of our favorites.

For the dough (converted)

Note: weight in parenthesis; weights are more accurate since cups/etc depend on type/quality of ingredient, temperature, etc.

6 ⅜ cups (800g) flour
½ cups (100g) unsalted butter
½ Cups (105g) sugar
3 eggs
1 cups (250mL) whole milk
2 tsp salt
2 ½ tbsp (22g) active dry yeast
¼ cup (5mL) vegetable oil
2 two-gallon plastic bags
A bucket of cold water

Instructions

- This dough is known as "diver's dough"
- Gently combine sugar, salt, and active yeast, crack three eggs into mixture, add 200mL of milk, mix well by hand.
- Add flour slowly and continue to mix.
- Add 100g of melted butter.
- Begin to knead the dough, if the dough is too tough then slowly add the remaining milk as needed, don't over knead!
- Pour 50mL of oil into one of the plastic bags and add the dough to it, put the bag into the other plastic bag and lower into the bucket of cold water, the room should be warm.
- Leave in the bag for an hour or an hour and a half, if it hasn't risen then leave for another half hour.
- Remove dough from bags and knead again to remove any bubbles.
- Cut in half and in half again.
- From each quarter you can either cut even pieces or use a glass to cut circles from it. Add your fillings, pinch closed, then flip over and apply glaze.

Potato filling:

Potatoes
Butter
Milks
Onions
Corn Oil

·

Instructions

- Prep potatoes like you would for mashed potatoes (peel, cut, salt the water, boil until soft, and mash).
- Add butter and milk to soften, depending on your tastebuds.
- Cut 1-2 onions in half rings, fry in corn oil until golden,
- Combine potatoes with onion and wait for them to cool before filling your piroshki.

Sour Cherry filing:

- Wait for sour cherry season!
- Use fresh pitted sour cherries (you can use frozen, but this is a pain in the butt).
- Add 2-3 Tbsp of sugar for 1lb pitted sour cherry
- Mix to combine, and put into sifter with a bowl underneath to allow the juices run, set juice aside.
- To the cherry add 1 Tbsp of flour or cornstarch (mix cornstarch with water first) to thicken the mixture.
- Fill your piroshki!
- For the remaining juice add a bit of water, sugar, and cornstarch (mix cornstarch with water first) bring this to a gentle simmer until it thickens.
- You can use this as a dipping sauce.

For glaze:

- Use two to three egg yolk with 2-3 tsp of milk to make a glaze.
- Let sit for 10-15 min.
- Bake in a preheated 375 oven for 35-40min until golden on top.

(Can't Live Without My) Котлеты Kotleti

Ideally, you ground the meat yourself. For pork you can use pork butt, and for beef, stew meat, otherwise use ground meat.

Ingredients

2lb ground pork
1lb ground beef (not lean, no more than 85% lean)
1 egg
1 large onion
3 cloves garlic
2 cups milk
stale baguette or french bread/rolls (use white bread)
salt and pepper to taste
vegetable oil to fry (ideally corn oil)
bay leaf
2 tbsp water

Instructions

- Cut bread into roughly 1-2in cubes, place in a bowl, and add milk.
- Soak your bread for about an hour, mixing every so often.
- Very finely chop onion and garlic.
- Combine meat, onion and garlic.
- Take your bread, and gently squeeze excess milk from it, but not so that they are fully dry.
- Add bread to the meat mixture and combine.
- Ensure that you don't over mix.
- Add egg, salt, and pepper, and stir to combine.
- Form a palm sized patty and fry in vegetable oil until golden brown on both sides.
- Move to a cast iron pan, add two tablespoons of water along with the oil used to fry.
- Add bay leaf.
- Cover and let simmer for 30 min.

THE LURE OF SWEET SWEET BIRCH TREE SAP
(берёзовый сок)

I dug around for kopecks—five I happily found.
Across the street I bravely walked, before I turned around...
What am I forgetting?
I wondered to myself.
To tell your parents of your plans.
I shrugged, and off I went.
To the corner store, where I had been, so many times before.
Meanwhile, the adults were frantic: how does a four-year-old just slip right out the door?
I walked across the street, confident and proud, never doubting for a moment that this might not be allowed.
I hand the clerk my kopecks, and in return, I drink...
Delicious birch tree sap juice, the most delicious thing!
This is how my parents discovered me, they seemed so very mad...
Is it because they haven't,
Had their birch tree sap juice yet?

FLAVORS I'LL NEVER FORGET

Watermelon in the summertime
Pistachio ice cream in Moscow
My first avocado
My first banana
Fresh-baked bread
Творог [tvorog] Soviet-style cottage cheese
сырки творожные [sirki tvorozhneye] cottage cheese dessert, whipped with sugar and vanilla, chocolate glazed
Freshly shucked corn

Flavors you'll never forget

_____
_____
_____
_____
_____
_____
_____
_____

TETYA POLYA'S FARM

> this is a story about **MISCHPACHA**, or family

Tetya Polya's* farm was at least a half day's journey from our own, though we may have traveled by bus or car or train. Of all the details I remember about her, the journey to her home is not one I can coax from my vault of childhood memories. I suspect the distance is why we didn't visit her more often, braving the trip only when there was a lot of work with which she needed help. She was older than my grandma and consequently seemed ancient to me, and she was all alone on that farm, save for her son. He was, the grown-ups whispered in confidence to one another, an alcoholic. To me, they simply said, "Ill. He's very ill." Even though by then I was as familiar with the sickly sweet smell of alcohol seeping through a man's pores as I was with the peonies that grew in my grandmother's garden.

> *FUN FACT
> Tetya Polya, in her advanced years, was known to consume only eggs- she ate ten a day!

Each discrete memory I have of my visits there, my mind has chosen to weave together like a spider's web, allowing me to crawl through them, starting from one point and always ending up somewhere unexpected, with no regard for chronology.

Her hut was tiny, and reminded me of the *Hut of Baba Yaga*, the home of the villainous grandmother witch, ever present in childhood fairytales. Tetya Polya seemed nothing like Baba Yaga. She was kind, spoke softly and always treated me to baked delicacies and fresh goat's milk. But I couldn't be sure that she did not turn wicked at nightfall. After all, she had a curious hump on her back, and always wore her kerchief tied tightly around her head making it impossible to check if there was a second pair of eyes hidden there. I soothed myself only with the knowledge that Tetya Polya's hut stood firmly bolted to the ground, and everyone knew a genuine Baba Yaga would have a house that stood upon chicken feet, ready at a moment's notice to dance with glee or turn about and chase a curious woodland hedgehog.

One early morning, I burst through the pasture, a pint-sized renegade charging full speed ahead. All around me, the birds spontaneously erupted into intricate chirps, harmonizing with one another, and I stopped in my tracks, marveling at the poetry of their work song.

One afternoon, we spent shucking corn, separating the criss-cross textured outer leaves to uncover the spun gold silk and perfect rows of kernels underneath. The discarded pile of silk growing larger and larger, daring me to jump in and bury my face inside the sweet earthy scent.

I remember I was in charge of sweeping the dirt floors . Ever the Sisyphean task, no matter how well I swept, I was always rewarded with a new layer of dirt below the old one.

I remember endless fields of wheat, row after row of dirt with potatoes growing underneath, and country animals of all sorts. Between the care-taking of the flora and fauna, and keeping the four of us fed, we never ran out of things to do, and days were filled from sun up to dusk. The work never seemed grueling, but instead, invigorating. The animals never a nuisance, but instead wildly animated. The lack of conveniences - a lack of water with the turn of the tap, or the ease of electricity, erased with the first taste of well water.

Could it really have been as idyllic as I recall? Or does my web of memories trick me into seeing it that way?

QUIZ

Quiz: Was your apartment Soviet-Chic (circa 1987):

- Rugs on the wall - *1 point for every room that had a rug on the wall*
- A cabinet of serving dishes - *3 points*
- A rotary phone - *5 points*
- Wall to wall book shelves - *3 points*
- A Samovar - *5 points*
- Tea glasses with podstakanniki (metal glass holders) - *4 points for a set*
- Big cleaver knife - *1 point*
- Miasnoi Molotok (meat tenderizing hammer)- *2 points*
- A piano (if you're fancy like that) - *3 points*
- Chessboard - *10 points*
- Record player - *2 points*
- A Vladimir Vysotsky record- *5 points*
- Playing cards - *2 points*
- Lotto - *3 points*
- Washing board - *5 points*
- Clothesline - *3 points*
- Rolling pin - *2 points*
- Valenki (galoshes) - *2 points*
- Ice skates - *5 points*
- Ushanka (hat with ear covering flaps) - *2 points*
- Embroidered napkins or tablecloth- 1 point for each
- Breadbox - *2 points*
- Nevalyashka (roly poly) doll - *3 points*
- Portrait of Lenin, Stalin, or any other communist party leader - *5 points per portrait*

If you have 30 points or more, congratulations you had yourself a Soviet Chic apartment (circa 1987)!

If you have less than 30 points, then you should have tried harder to be Soviet chic.

GOODBYE AMERICA, LONGING TO LEAVE

> This is a story about **MISHIGAS** or craziness. Specifically about the craziness of immigrating.

I could never have imagined it without a little help.

In my child's mind, I pictured a mound of sand, a palm tree (with coconuts!), and my grandparents clinging to it to survive. I spent weeks fretting about how we would swim there and alternatively about how we would all fit!

Thanks to a couple of photographs and some letters sent across the great ocean, a new vision began to take shape. No longer picturing a tiny speck of an island, I now imagined towering buildings, lush landscapes with trees as far as the eye could see, strange-looking birds, even stranger-looking people, and a bridge made of solid gold!

I longed for it. This place I had never been to. This country I had only read about. This magical land with fruit in the winter time, jeans in all sizes, and no lines at the store counter!

"A Barbie there costs six dollars!"

"That doesn't sound like much, I bet you could save for a few in no time."

"Will you promise to send us back one?"

I promised. *"Of course!"* I promised them all. I'd write letters and learn English and send them all back Beatles cassette-tapes and Barbies and Bubble gum. I was so excited, I could hardly stand it!

"When will we leave?

"Soon, so soon. You won't even have to start school because we're leaving any day now."

I waited patiently.

The weeks turned into months. My friends all started first grade. I roamed the playground alone until the babies would be let out of nursery school. I'd organize them into a merry band of thieves and send them on daring missions to the corner store. *"I'm going to America, and you're going to miss me so much. You'll cry even!"*

I told my pint-sized pack of hooligans.

Each night, I packed my suitcase, folding my clothes neatly and carefully selecting the two toys and three books my parents said I could take with me. "*Any day now,*" I would tell myself, giddy with anticipation.

The school year ended, and a new one was beginning. Dreading another year of boredom, I begged to go, and this time my parents agreed. Every week it seemed a classmate would leave for America, for Israel, or Germany.

But still, we stayed.

"*Any day,*" I would keep telling myself, but I stopped packing.

My aunt, uncle, and cousins moved out of our apartment. From twelve people, there were only five of us left. It was quiet, and the bathroom was always available when you needed it. Where was the fun in that?

There were rations for milk and soap. One day I went to the corner store, and they were out of bread. So was the store in the town square and the 'super' store down by the movie theater.

My grandma called to say the earth shook over there, and she had broken her leg.

I started having nightmares. America was a small island again, but the ground was unstable, and the palm tree split down the middle.

I would play this one song, the lyrics "Goodbye America, though I've never laid eyes on you" would always make me cry. I'd get myself worked up to a state bordering on hysteria and then, finally, sleep.

My great-grandmother, the woman who raised me, had a stroke and died.

I no longer cared if we ever left for America.

By the time we landed at 11:15pm on January 11th, 1991 at San Francisco International Airport, I barely even registered it; that, indeed, my whole world had shifted.

*FUN FACT
*the song Гудбай, Америка *Goodbye America is by Nautilius Pompilius, a Soviet band*

BREAKFAST BUFFET

this is a story with some low key **KVETCHING** *or complaining*

This is what I remember about the day(s) we actually immigrated to America.

I vaguely remember saying goodbye to my relatives, traveling by train to Moscow, then taking a cab to the Moscow airport. **[Editor's note: 'vaguely remembered' is not a memoir worthy mentioning!]**

My first real memory is of the next airport we ended up in. It should have been on American soil, but it was not! The way I remember it is that we had to stop because of a fueling issue, but this memory has not been corroborated by my parents.

[Editor's note: what did we just discuss? accuracy is of utmost importance in a memoir!]

I remember sitting in the plastic orange airport seats, with dull overhead lighting, with lots of tense adults all around me, particularly my parents. They were chain smoking. Or did I make that up? **[Editor's note: you are becoming what we call in the business, an unreliable narrator.]** We had brought a book with us, I believe it was intended as a present for someone's child in America, but it was all I had in the form of entertainment, so I carefully turned the pages and tried hard not to leave any marks. In it, I reread my favorite story, the boy Nils whisked away by swans to the magical land of Laplandia. We were in the airport for what felt like hours, my parents attempting to communicate with the help of an English phrasebook to the airline representatives to figure out what was happening.

The next thing I remember is that the airline decided that they could not fly out that day, and we were to be put up in a hotel room for the night. We drove for about a half hour, on the cleanest and emptiest road I had ever been on, through a landscape that was pure fairytale. Rolling green hills, bright blue skies, and sunshine, not a speck of litter on the highway. I might have even seen a sheep or two dotting the hills. I thought that I was in the magical land of Laplandia. Close enough, I was in Ireland. **[Editor's note: finally some halfway decent storytell-**

ing. Adequate job kid!]

Where was I? Oh right! We arrived at a modest but very clean hotel (a Holiday Inn, my mom supplies) and were instructed to order room service.

How can I properly convey to you the experience of being in a hotel room (for the very first time in my life), picking up a telephone and having food that you did not prepare yourself (and more importantly did not stand in three different lines to procure) arrive a mere 30 minutes later? Imagine an adorable (slightly underfed) cartoon animal with eyes (as big as saucers), a mouth frozen in the shape of an O, perpetually blinking its enormous eyelashes gratefully as they take in every detail of what seems like a dream unfolding right in front of its eyes.

The food arrived on a cart and was wheeled into our room. My dad lifted the metal cover off our plates..

Hold on, can I just pause here for a moment. A metal cover for your food? To keep it warm for you to enjoy? This was pure sorcery!

...to reveal yellowish orange sticks of fried potatoes, a piece of meat (that I was later taught was a hamburger), and alfalfa sprouts.

Oh man, alfalfa sprouts. The audacity of a vegetable existing purely for decoration like that, it still gets me.

This was the most exciting conclusion of the most exciting day that I had experienced up to this point in my life.

Until the next morning.

Allow me to pause for a moment and explain that in Russian folklore there exists the concept of a magical tablecloth скатерть-самобранка [skatert-samobranka] that one must simply unfurl to reveal a plethora of food that is constantly magically replenished for you. **[Editor's note: say more about this, this actually seems interesting.]**

Well, the next morning we came downstairs to a dining room and I came face to face with an actual real life skatert-samobranka, in the form of a breakfast buffet. There were few things I recognized on this buffet and was very nearly too intimidated to make a selection, until I found a familiar looking container of flakes made of corn (I think you might know them as Corn Flakes) and proceeded to pour some into a bowl. There was a jug of milk right next to this container and a hotel wait staff member indicated to me that I should pour the milk into the bowl with the flakes. I was dubious but I didn't want to offend anyone so I poured the milk in and sat down at my table to eat it.

Imagine for a moment, if you can, that your whole childhood you have been eating these flakes of corn, corn flakes if you will, as a dry snack – в сухомятку[v suhomatku] as we say in Russian,) and it has never (would never) occur to you to pour milk on them! And now here you are tasting that first magical spoonful of slightly soggy, yet also crunchy flakes of goodness? Ah reader, I wish I could let you taste that first spoonful with me.

After breakfast, we were due to drive back to the airport and this I simply could not understand. Why? Why were we leaving this magical place? It's so clean. There's fried potatoes, and teeny tiny vegetables that appear under metal-covered trays in your room and as many flakes with corn as your stomach can hold!

Why would anyone give up this sure thing for the promise of an unknown land called America?

Would there even be fried potatoes and flakes of corn there?

I was about to find out.

[Editor's note: bit of a cliche using a cliffhanger here but I guess I'll allow it.]

A COMEDY OF ERRORS

*this is a **HOHMA**, a funny story*

When we first immigrated, I would argue that the single biggest adjustment we had to make was not learning English, but learning supermarkets. From waiting in line for each type of ingredient (bread, fruits & veggies, meat, dairy) to having everything accessible and seemingly always in season was dizzying.

Living in San Francisco meant we were particularly spoiled. We had your typical supermarkets (Safeway and such), corner store groceries and ethnic groceries (see: twelve separate Russian groceries within twenty blocks of each other.)

But we had limitations. Cost was obviously a huge consideration but there were other challenges. As soon as I got here I underwent allergy testing only to discover that everything was a possible allergy trigger for me and thus began a many months long elimination diet with us removing a laundry list of things from my diet and reintroducing them to see if there's a reaction.

I couldn't eat dairy for example, so my parents bought the first dairy free "milk" option they came across at the supermarket and that's how I came to eat my generic cornflakes with Mocha Mix.

Mocha Mix in case you didn't know was made of...

Water, Corn Syrup, Partially Hydrogenated Soybean Oil (Adds a Trivial Amount of Saturated Fat), Contains 2% or Less of the Following: Distilled Monoglycerides, Soy Protein Isolate, Dipotassium Phosphate, Polysorbate 60, Sodium Stearoyl Lactylate, Salt, Artificial Flavor, Beta Carotene (Color).

Go ahead and try it for yourself, I'll just wait here with a bucket if (when) you need it.

LoST iN TRaNSLaTioN

> this is another **HOHMA** (joke) for you

Upon immigrating my dad worked three times harder than your average Joe just trying to get hired anywhere. Over the years he tried his hand at any number of jobs. He worked at a paint mixing plant, he was a bus boy and then a waiter (and eventually head waiter!), he even tried to get a job at a massage parlor downtown (he's a talented self taught masseuse) but unfortunately it was a downtown 'massage parlor' so he didn't get the job.

One day he happened upon a neighborhood Taqueria (Mexican fast food restaurant) owned by a fellow former Soviet immigrant (I know, I know, I wouldn't have bet on odds like that either) and he quickly found himself as a business partner to this fellow fella.

Being a business partner of a small restaurant meant that you did a little of everything: prep in the kitchen, janitorial services, ordering food, and anything else that needed doing.

One such job that fell to him was to re-do the menus. This was the early 90s, and having plastic stick-on letters on a menu board was all the rage. I found him in the middle of this job, painstakingly removing the plastic letters and adhering them to the plastic menu board, and right in the middle of that menu were the words "HOT INTERCOURSES."

He didn't know the word for appetizers but figured that going for a literal translation was the best option. And so, appetizers became the hot dishes that are served before the main course is served, or hot inter-courses.

> *FUN FACT
>
> I experienced a similar translation snafu when learning Spanish. Having blundered over something I announced to my classmates that I was so embarazada! Or 'pregnant' in Spanish.

COVETiNG (FLUORESCENT CURLY CUES OF PERFECTiON)

> this is another story with some low key **KVETCHING** or complaining

As any immigrant child or child of immigrants will tell you, the fastest way to spot someone that's fresh off the boat (or plane, or what have you) is by what they bring to school for lunch. I guess you could say I lucked out in this regard, as I was never smelly-lunch-girl. I was her second cousin: weird-lunch-girl.

My grandparents really tried to help me fit in by buying me what they understood to be American food, like hot dogs, but they could never get it quite right. So while they might have bought me hot dogs they neglected to buy hot dog buns so I would end up with hot dogs sliced in half and in half again stuck between two slices of bread with not even a smear of mayonnaise to help the medicine go down.

Eventually, I took over my own lunch preparations and my lunches became the most American lunch possible (read: The most American lunch that we could afford) - two slices of white Iron Kids bread (the marketing was genius, am I right) with two slices of Oscar Mayer bologna (ok so maybe it wasn't actually name-brand bologna but that's the beautiful thing about bologna, you can't tell if it's name brand by looking at a naked slice) and a Martinelli's apple juice.

The trouble was, my parents refused to buy any of the other paraphernalia that would have rounded out these meals and made them truly American. I longed for a bag of Doritos or a packet of Fruit Gushers, and sometimes I even dared to dream of a Capri Sun that you poked through with a straw or Kool-Aid served in a plastic squeeze bottle. None of these passed my parents' test of affordable and nutritious lunch content. And thus my lunches were spent in envy of my friends....

The bell rings, and we trickle down like tributaries to the lower courtyard. This is where the girl's group sits. The boys sit further down the fence in the corner by the entrance. After we eat, the boys will merge into us.

We never eat together. I don't know why, but it suits everyone just fine.

Now comes the part I hate, each girl reaches into her backpack and pulls out a brown paper bag or an insulated plain lunchbox—no cartoon characters, we're not children—and begins to sort through the contents.

Multi-layered sandwiches with sliced deli meats and fancy cheeses: California pepper jack, provolone, Wisconsin cheddar. Always a piece of lettuce, sometimes tomatoes too.

Shiny packaging pulled open to reveal crackers, ham, and cheese, all in perfect miniature! These you can stack, two, four, six at a time—towers of culinary and geometric accomplishment.

Mallory pulls out a thermos with soup. Soup! Can you imagine? Chicken noodle or minestrone, maybe even clam chowder, lovingly ladled and kept warm by the magic metal container.

JJ got a pickle! A whole pickle! She is so lucky.

Stephanie procures a crinkly bag, opens it slowly, oh these are my favorite! Fluorescent curly cues of perfection. Their orange powder, guaranteed to stay on your fingers well into fifth period.

Now the floor is open for negotiations.

Doritos Cool Ranch are swapped for Lay's Sour Cream and Onion. Half a turkey on whole wheat for tuna salad (with relish) on Dutch Crunch.

Sure, that makes sense.

Hostess cupcakes for Fruit Gushers.

That's just stupid! Seven perfect squiggles atop chocolaty sponge cake with a vanilla cream filling for a measly ten or twelve rubbery fruit flavored drops? Some of them flavors you don't even like? You should at least hold out for Fruit RollUp, that you can wrap around your finger, pointing and licking to your heart's content.

The girls buying lunch that day don't even participate. And why should they? They've hit the jackpot, a lunch of your own choosing. Piping hot pizza or greasy chow mein. Maybe even nachos with pickled jalapenos, and It's Its for dessert!

Uncharacteristically, I stay quiet. I have nothing to contribute. Nothing for the trading floor, no pocket money for a stray Ring Pop. And my lunch? Never an element of surprise.

I know exactly what my foil pouch holds: Iron Kids bread and bologna with a Martinelli's apple juice to drink. I know because I packed it myself. I've packed it myself ever since I stopped eating the school lunch in fifth grade. No sides. No pickles. Certainly, no dessert.

They are finishing up now, Lee's already singing "Tommy played piano like a kid out in the rain, then he lost his leg in Dallas he was dancing with a train"

And just like that my gluttonous girlfriends have had their fill and begin offering up the remnants, does anyone want this?

Sometimes I bite. Well, I'll take it if you're just going to throw it away. Cool, nonchalant, whatever.

If it's something amazing, I'll make them dare me to eat it.

I bet I can eat that french fry dipped in ice cream!

Ewwww no way, do it! Do it! Ooooh nasty!

I watch as at least three bites of sandwich are discarded, chip crumbs are thoughtlessly wiped from jackets, a half-eaten apple shoved back into a backpack.

But I always have to let some of it go. You can't look too eager. That's just embarrassing.

"Cinnamon and sugary and softly spoken lies you never know just how you look through other people's eyes."[3]

---

3 "Pepper" by Butthole Surfers

I DiDNT BECOME A SUPERMODEL, BUT I DiD gET To TRY A RooT BEER FLOAT

Another **MANTSA** *little piece of gossip for you*

I was discovered at the City College of San Francisco.

That's right.

When I was nine years old, I accompanied my aunt to her English class at City College of San Francisco. One of her classmates, who was married to a photographer, took one look at me and convinced my aunt that her husband simply **had** to photograph me.

Apparently I had the face for modeling.

This fed right into my fantasy, the one where a talent scout happens to wander into my local elementary school and plucks me out of obscurity to star as a spirited young heroine in a big a Hollywood movie. This fantasy was possibly less about fame and fortune and more about getting my classmates to see me as something other than a weird lunch-smelling, non-brand-name shoes-wearing, cootie-girl.

I didn't even realize that photographers normally charge hundreds of dollars for the pleasure of providing headshots for young hopefuls. But because my aunt was a friend of his wife's - he took my pictures for free.

I remember they had an enormous backyard, I didn't even know houses in San Francisco had backyards! First, he shot pictures of me dressed in the clothes that I was wearing, a simple black T-shirt and jeans. Then he dug through his wife's closet to provide a white button-up shirt for me. She took a spray bottle and misted my hair thoroughly so that it was wet and could be styled.

As it turned out I loved getting my picture taken, I enjoyed the hour-plus-long session with zero complaints and did everything that he asked of me. He had his own kids so he knew how to keep the shoot interesting and how to communicate with me. And when we 'wrapped' I even got to eat pizza and try a brand new American beverage—root beer! With ice cream in it!

After a few weeks, he had us look through the photos and indicated his favorite one to be printed into a headshot photo with which to approach modeling agencies for representation. It was one of the photos in which my hair was wet and styled, and I looked like a very slender fourteen-year-old.

It took my parents a few months to prioritize getting these images printed, but eventually we found ourselves at a modeling agency in downtown San Francisco. Unfortunately in the time that it took for us to take the photos and sit down with these people who held my fate in their hands, the puberty train had truly arrived for me and the agents were faced with a creature trapped in the most unattractive transition period between "not a girl not yet a woman."

And that was the end of my modeling career.

But at least I got to try a rootbeer float.

At Rochambeau playground is where I spent most of my days...

THE ONE WHERE MY MOM BAKES CAKES*

Good natured teasing is what led us to this predicament.

The predicament where every day for the last two weeks my mother has baked a cake.

The same cake.

Intent on perfecting this one culinary masterpiece.

We've got cake in the breadbox, cake in the oven, cake in the refrigerator, cake cooling on the fire escape.

My grandmother took home three. My aunt took two. Our immediate neighbors have all been gifted one each.

And yet the cakes keep coming.

"*You never cook or bake anything,*" we foolishly teased her.

"*Unless you count salads,*" I quipped, adding salt to the wound*.

The look in her eyes said, "I'll show you."

The next fourteen days, she waged a battle against our willpower.

The first cake we praised. "*Wow Mom, it's fantastic. Look what you can do when you set your mind to it!*"

The second cake we diligently compared and contrasted with the first. "*Yes it IS more moist. I CAN really taste the lemon zest.*"

The third, we chuckled.

The fourth, we invited our relatives and shared our bounty.

By day five, we were concerned.

> *FUN FACT
>
> If you guessed that this story title as written in the style of a Friends episode title, you'd be correct! As we say in Russian: **возми печенье с полки** [vozmi pechnye s polki] or take a cookie off the shelf to reward yourself.

> *PROVERB ALERT
>
> this saying in Russian is **не сыпь мне соль на рану** [ne syp' mne sol' na ranu]

By the ninth, we considered an intervention.
But by the thirteenth, we accepted our fate.
Cake.
It's what's for dinner.
Today, tomorrow, and until the end of time.

The moral of the cake story...

Is there anything more obnoxious than a snot-nosed kid's grievances against their own mother? A kid who can't tell you anything about their mother as a human being (not her favorite book or color or meal) but can list (unprompted) all of the ways in which their mother has failed them that day and since the beginning of time. As children, our (perfectly developmentally appropriate) perception is that the entire world - and especially our parents - exist simply to fulfill our every wish and desire. It's difficult to even conceive of parents being fully formed humans with their own thoughts and feelings and world views that might be as valid as our own (what with our cultivating it for a good ten or twelve years?)

Having been the child in this particular scenario, I can only say, Mom, I'm sorry. I'm sorry I failed to fully appreciate the gifts you bring to our family (and they are plentiful) and instead held you to standards molded largely by American sitcoms in which the mother somehow does three full-time jobs, including cooking a meal from scratch every night.

Were my own children to accuse me of not contributing enough to our family I don't know that my response would be to bake cakes for them! Lucky for dad and I, what started as taunting turned out to be uncovering a hidden talent. These days my mom has a repertoire of cakes that she bakes for special and everyday occasions and we never ever take her for granted anymore.

The end.
Amen.

STORY SNACKS: KIPPERS, FETTUCCINE ALFREDO, KETCHUP AND KIX

Kippers

For a brief moment in time when we all first immigrated, we stuck together in small family clusters. My mom and dad and I lived with my mom's parents (Liliya and Vova).

My grandma's parents (my great-grandparents Manya and Misha) lived with their grown grandkids and their great grandkids. And because my grandparents were working and my parents were hard at work finding work, I had very little adult supervision.

That first summer in America, I ended up spending a lot of time with my great grandma and my second cousins – two rambunctious, obnoxious boys who spent their days playing video games and watching the same two Disney movies on repeat.

They had already spent more of their lives in America than in the Soviet Union, so their food choices were as exotic to me as the food my great-grandma served me was to them. Case in point? Their snack of choice was pizza and mine was black bread and sprats: a small smoked fish with a pungent aroma and a delicious flavor. I still have a soft spot in my heart for those little golden brown fishes that you can pick up at any Russian grocery store.

Fettuccine Alfredo

I was nine years old when I decided to make an American meal from scratch*. I'd heard a lot about Fettuccine Alfredo, what with the never-ending Olive Garden commercials on TV, and I knew that this should be my first foray into following a recipe and making a meal for myself. My parents had a subscription to Cooking Light and from its pages I selected a fettuccine alfredo recipe.

> *FUN FACT
>
> *And by this I mean a meal that required cooking because by age nine I was already the proud of inventor of chocolate toast: a creation that involved bread (preferably IronKids bread) butter, and powdered QuikMix*

Unfortunately, I quickly discovered I was missing some key ingredients, mainly fettuccine pasta and parmesan cheese. So I improvised by cooking capellini and making a cheddar-based sauce. I remember the color being bright orange and the consistency being quite lumpy.

My mom tried a bite out of politeness, and I stubbornly ate two bowls before admitting defeat.

To this day, I'm a rebel and have trouble following recipes. Even when we have all the required ingredients, I often add my own spin on things just for fun.

Ketchup (and Kix)

My childhood best friend, Stella, lived four blocks away, and in the summer between fifth and sixth grade, I essentially lived at her house. This meant I partook in many meals (and snacks) at her house. She was three years older than me, fourteen to my eleven when we met, and therefore much more sophisticated in the kitchen than I was.

Here is a complete list of everything Stella ever cooked for me:
- Spaghetti and ketchup
- Oven baked frozen french fries and ketchup
- Cereal* ketchup optional

*though this was really less her cooking and more me reaching for an opened box of Kix

(Kix – kid tested, mother approved) the box was always left open because she liked them stale and munching as quietly as possible from the bottom of the trundle bed as I waited for her to wake up.

Her repertoire in the kitchen might be the reason she always preferred eating out. Thanks to her, I discovered the miracle of dim sum and, more specifically, char sui buns and har gow (aka bbq pork buns and shrimp dumplings), always accompanied by Coca Cola. She also had an eclectic taste in snacks—her favorite was dried squid!

HOW TO BE A GOOD HOST/GUEST

And now darling reader, we've come to the very end. As my final bit of hospitality I'll share with you both how to be a good guest and a good host to the Soviet people in your life!

Every Soviet immigrant I know could feed a group of thirty at a moment's notice because of how they stock their pantry, fridge, and freezer. So if you unexpectedly have guests drop by make sure to have stocked Soviet style so you can be an excellent host on a moment's notice.

Here are some ideas for you:

Pantry - canned sprats, canned fish in tomato sauce, crackers, olives, potatoes

Fridge - pickled herring, pickled cabbage, pickles or tomatoes, dill, mayo, eggs*, bread and butter

Freezer - vodka, pelmeni, leftover stew from when you made too much

> ***FUN FACT**
>
> *In America people joke that if the food runs out at a party we can always order pizza, in a Soviet household the joke is we can always make an omelet.*

If all else fails just serve tea and the sweets your guests have brought you.

Speaking of sweets your guests have brought you...

Rules for guest behavior in a former Soviet immigrant household:

- Never come empty-handed (always bring something, sweets are always acceptable)

- Never open a Soviet person's refrigerator
- Remove your shoes - the host should offer you тапочки [tapochki] slippers
- Always accept seconds—it's a tricky balance between eating everything offered but leaving enough, so they don't feel like they made too little, be prepared/pace yourself
- Compliment the chef!

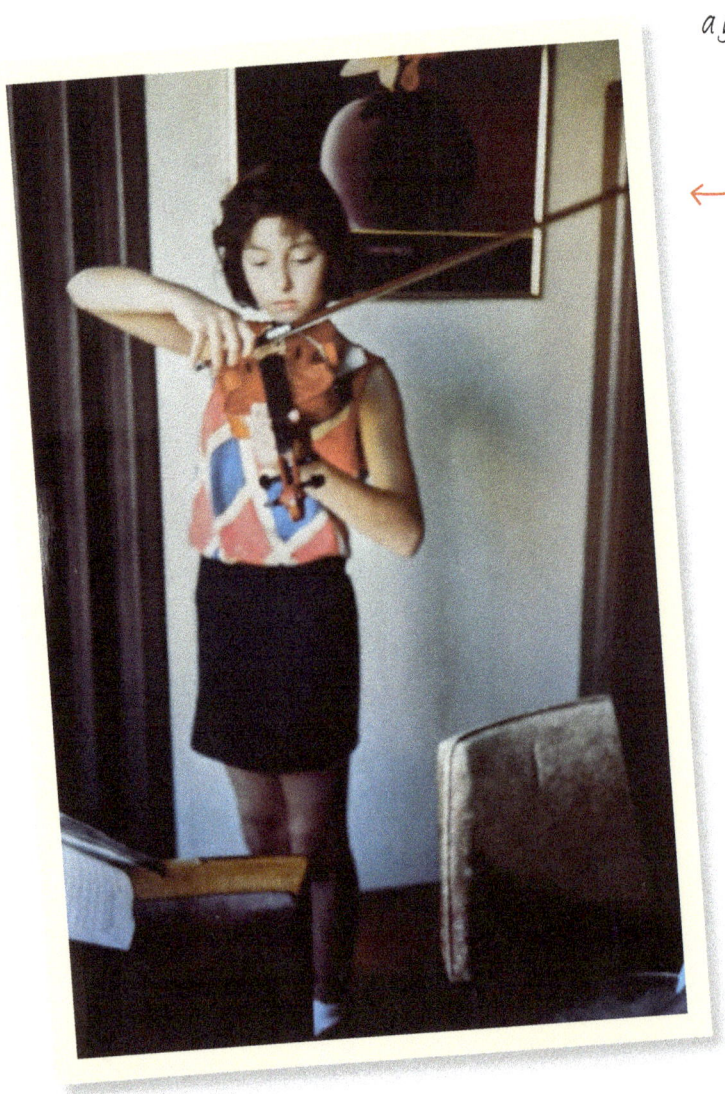

how NOT to be a good guest/host

CONCLUSION/EPILOGUE

Why is celebration so important? Why is coming together to break bread so important? Why did companies like Google develop an entire food program dedicated to the idea that when people come together and eat together, they will share stories and connect in a way that they were previously unable to?

Because when you come together for a meal, be it an everyday breakfast or a special occasion ice cream with your children, or even an elaborate 50th birthday party complete with themed tables that represent every single milestone in your life, it allows you to share something of yourself. It allows you to know that when you look across the table, you are not alone.

The ethos of "until the last pickle" is that we celebrate together. And it means that we value taking care of the people we welcome into our homes and into our lives. It says that even though the pantry is almost empty and even though we may not know where that next meal is coming from, this is the moment that we have together with one another. Whether we are having a great time at that moment or a shit time because we're grieving and we're crying. No matter the circumstance, no matter the reason, "until the last pickle means," let's do it. Let's cut up that pickle. Let's take that leap of faith. We don't know what tomorrow is going to bring, but today, we have the ability to taste the complex flavors of life.

And after thirty years in America, we are all re-examining our relationship to what is in our pantries, what is served at the table, and how we express love and care.

Any armchair psychologist will tell you that there is a pretty obvious connection between the scarcity we experienced in the Soviet Union and the indulgence and excess that this led to in the United States.

The contrast between the hoops that we had to get through to get something as basic as food on the table with the simplicity of walking into a corner store and being able to find almost everything you need is stark. And toggling between the two may have created some whiplash.

And yes, in a culture where food is scarce, where food is love, and where every single celebration has a special meal/ dish/ dessert attached to it. It might just manifest into love handles. I don't know why we call them love-handles, but I'm pretty sure it just means that more love was given to you, and now you have extra to handle.

So the answer to the question: Why do we celebrate?

Because we can.

Because we get to.

Because we can never underestimate the gift of having the freedom to celebrate the holidays of our choosing, the blessing to have the people we love around us, and the relative ease with which we can procure food!

And ironically, these days, we spend more time arguing over what to cull from our tables rather than what to add. It seems we have all (finally) had our fill.

ACKNOWLEDGMENTS

To everyone that fed and nourished me while I wrote this book.

MY FAMILY

My parents - Marina and Peter, who helped to fill in the gaps of my childhood memories and continue to feed me even though I am technically a grown ass adult. Bonus thanks for their party spreads which are truly EPIC!

My grandma, Babushka Liliya, for sharing her secret recipes, stories, and photos with me.

My mother in law, Yelena, for painstakingly translating her recipes for me and for continuing to make us sour cream cake even though it is obviously a pain in the tuchus to do so.

My aunt Natasha and her family for being fantastic hosts and continuing to throw fun family celebrations for me to attend.

My husband, Stan.
One of the ways he happens to express his love is by making me tea and snacks- which couldn't be more perfect for this voraciously hungry and frequently lazy gal. Thanks babe, I could do it without you but it would be a lot less fun.

And of course my children, who are ultimately my reason for doing any of this.

MY FRIENDS AND COLLEAGUES WHO NURTURE ME IN SO MANY WAYS.

Specifically, the Hivery's Grace Kraaijvanger and Amber Allen-Peirson for their support and collaboration. My Hivery incubator crew aka "the Hatchlings" and most especially Rachel Hebert for her willingness to provide design feedback. To my "biz besties" Freesia Lee and Jess Coleman, thank you for your tough love and endless good ideas.

My homies in the Only Children's Club: Vika Balanov for all of her copy edits and katching alL of the spellling misssstakes. Gaby Makstman for her ongoing support and friendship.

And Natalya Vaksman for always being available for a pharmaceutical consultation during this stressful process (and for being my friend.)

The rest of my homies: Vivian Chu and Kelly Meehan for the plethora of childhood memories and plenty in our grown up years too. Lana Gulden, little sister I never wanted but now can't live without. Inna Meklin for letting me play life coach whenever I want. And to the best bosses turned friends Aleya Harris and Kellyx Nelson for their ongoing support in daily life, a text from you can change my day around.

My childhood best friend Stella L., may her memory be a blessing. Thank you for all of the meals - spaghetti, bbq pork buns with Coca Cola, Kix cereal, and many more. Thank you for being the very best friend a girl could ever ask for. We never did get to write our screenplay together but this is pretty cool right?

Everyone participating in the audiobook but especially my voiceover (VO) accountability pals! The OG VO accountability crew Nina Greeley, Lynda Kluck, Stephanie Shumunes, Emiko Susilo and the incomparable Susan Vlahos. The VO accountability crew full of everyone younger than me: Julie Hancock, Sarah Norris, Lucy Parkinson and Laura Quiambao.

Thank you to everyone else in the audiobook, your willingness to just jump in and play is inspirational! Bridget Maguire Colton, Roni Gallimore, Steve Fait (also our awesome engineer), Shannon Kealey, Diane Hayes, Yinka Ladeinde, Amy Larson, Tina Morasco, Tom Pinto, Amy Stafford, Lisa Star, and the insanely talented Danny Scott - my journey in voiceover would not be same without you buddy!

The book production team of Get It Done Productions: Lucy Giller for all of your beautiful design work, Woz Flint for steering this book ship amidst turbulent waters. Andwr Fox for being the kindest editor. Lindsey Smith for your marketing brilliance and Alexandra Franzen for your quiet and steady guidance over these last nine years, it's pretty awesome to have you in my corner.

REFERENCES

Smith, Alison K., *Cabbage and Caviar: A History of Food in Russia* London: Reaktion Books, 2021.

GLOSSARY

Yiddish

Kvetching *complaining*
кишен тухис [kishen tuchis] *kiss my butt*
манса [mantsa] *gossip*
мишигас [mishigas] *craziness, madness, silliness*
мишпуха [mishpucha] *you people, family, chosen or given (often spelled as mishpacha)*
нахис [nahis] *blessings, joy*
тухис [tuchis] *butt*
хохма [hohma] *joke, anecdote, witty story*
цурис [tsuris] *troubles, challenges, hard times*

Russian

березовый сок [berezovyy sok] *birch tree sap juice*
бистро [bistro] *cafe*
блат [blat] *favors*
Блинчики [blinchiki] *crepes*
борщ [borscht] *cabbage soup*
Бриллиантовая Рука [brillantovaya ruka] *The Diamond Arm*
булавка [bulavka] *pin*
бульон [bullion] *broth*
Буратино и малвина [buratino and malvina] *two dolls based on the Russian version of Pinocchio*
быстро [bistro] *quickly*

в сухомятку [v suhomatku] *to eat something dry*

вафельный торт [vaffelniy tort] *waffle cake*

Винегрет [vinegret] *salad Vinegret*

вода [voda] *water*

встречаться [vstrechatsa] *to meet*

второе [vtoroye] *second course*

второй завтрак [vtoroy zavtrak] *second breakfast*

выбросили [viebrosiliye] *thrown away*

голубцы [golubtsi] *cabbage stuffed with beef and rice*

гость [gost] *guest*

гробки [grobki] *graves*

дают [dayut] *giving*

Дед Мороз Vded moroz] *Grandpa Frost*

дедушка [dedushka] *grandfather*

День защи́тника Оте́чества [den zaschetnika otchestva] *Defender of the Fatherland Day*

дефицит [defitzit] *deficit products*

докторская колбаса [doktorskaya kolbasa] *doctor's kielbasa*

домовая кухня [domovaya kuhnya] *home kitchen*

достать [do-stat] *to acquire*

дружила [druzhila] *was friends with*

дружить [druzhit] *to be friends*

дурак [durak] *fool*

ёлочка [yolachka] *pine tree (Christmas tree)*

за здоровье [za zdorovye] *Typically a toast said to health*

за маму [za mamu] *for Mom*

за папу [za papu] *for Dad*

завтрак [zavtrak] *breakfast*

закуска [zakuska] *appetizer*

закуски [zakuski] *appetizers*

Ирония судьбы или с лёгким паром [roniya sudbi ili s lekhim parom] *'The irony of fate, or enjoy your bath.'*

капуста [kapusta] *cabbage*

161

Карнавальная ночь [karnavalnaya noch] *Carnival night*

кафетерия [kafeteriya] *cafeteria*

кекс [keks] *cake*

Киевский [Kyivskyi] *Kyiv cake*

Книга о вкусной и здоровой пище [Kniga o vkusnoi i zdorovoi pishche] *The book of tasty and healthy food*

колбаса [kolbasa] *cold cuts*

коммуналка [komunnalka] *communal kitchens*

компания [kompaniya] *group of friends*

компот [kompot] *fruit compote was self service*

комсомол [komsomol] *is a syllabic abbreviation of the political youth organization in the Soviet Union - Коммунистический Союз Молодёжи [Kommunisticheskiy Soyuz Molodyozhi]*

комсомольская свадьба [komsomolskaya svadba] *a civil wedding*

котлеты [kotleti] *meat patties*

красная коляска [krasnaya kolyaska] *red stroller*

красный день календаря [krasniy den kalendarya] *red calendar days*

купить [kupit] *buy*

лото [lotto] *bingo*

любительская колбаса [luybitelskaya kolbasa] *favorite kielbasa*

Масленица [Maslenitsa] *a holiday where crepes are made*

н.з. | en ze| nz| *an abbreviation for неприкосновенный запас [ne prekosnoveney zapas] your untouchable supply*

на вынос [na vinos] *to go*

найти [nayti] *to find*

Наполеон [Napoleon] *Napoleon cake*

непрерывная рабочая неделя [nepreryvnaya rabochaya nedelya] *a continuous production week, commonly referred to as непрерывка [nepreryvka]*

Новый Год [Novoi god] *New Year's*

обед [obed] *lunch in the Soviet union, used as dinner in America*

общество чистых тарелок [obchestvo chistih tarelok] *the society of clean plates*

освежать [osvezhat] *to refresh*

Павлова [Pavlova] *meringue cake*

Пасха [Pascha] *Orthodox Easter*

Пасха [paskha] *Easter*

пельмени [pelmini] *dumpligs*

пельменная [pel'mennaya] *a store that sold dumplings*

первое [pervoye] *first course*

пирожки [piroshki] *baked or fried buns with a variety of fillings*

пирожковая [pirozhkovaya] *a store that sold pirozhki*

по блату [po blatu] *through favors*

полудник [poludnik] *a mid day snack*

полуфабрикат [polu fabrikat] *partially prepared food*

презерватив [preservative] *which means condom (not jam)*

пятая графа [pyatoya grafa] *the fifth line of your passport application in the Soviet Union*

ресторан [restoran] *restaurant*

Рождество [Rozhdestvo] *a Russian Orthodox holiday celebrating the birth of Christ*

с именинником [s immeninikom] *congratulations for your loved one's birthday*

Салат Оливье [salat olivye] *salad Olivye*

сало [salo] *lard*

свадебный генерал [svadebniy general] *wedding general*

сглазить [zglazit] *to look at someone and cause them ill*

секрет фаршированной рыбы [sekret farshorivonay ribye] *the secret of stuffed fish*

секс *sex*

Селёдка с картошкой [seledka s kartoshkoi] *pickled Herring and mashed potatoes*

сырки творожные [sirki tvorozhneye] *cottage cheese dessert, whipped with sugar and vanilla, chocolate glazed*

скатерть-самобранка [skatert-samobranka] *a magical tablecloth*

сметанник [smetannik] *sour cream cake*

Снегурочка [snegurachka] *Snowflake*

Старый Новый Год [stariy novoi god]   *Old New Years*

столовая [stolovaya]   *canteen*

сухой закон [suhoi zakon]   *dry laws*

тапочки [tapochki]   *slippers*

творог [tvorog]   *cottage cheese*

тоска [toska]   *a uniquely Russian word that means both longing, nostalgia, and suffering all in one*

третье [treteye]   *third course*

угостить [ugostit]   *to serve your guests something special*

ужин [uzhin]   *supper*

украшают [ukrashayut]   *decorating a dish*

ухаживали за мной [uhazhivaly za mnoi]   *took care of me*

ухаживать [uhazhivanya]   *to take care of*

хлеб и соль [hleb i sol']   *bread and salt*

хлебосольство [khlebosolstvo]   *hospitality*

ходить в гости [hodit v gosti]   *visiting*

Холодное [holodnoye]   *aspic*

шестидневка [shestidnevka]   *six-day production week*

юбилей [yubiley]   *anniversary*

PROVERBS/SAYINGS IN ORDER OF APPEARANCE

before the start of any meal we all wish each other **приятного аппетита** [priyatnovo appetita] or Bon appetit

"пословица" poslovitsa or **"поговорка"** pogovorka- while in English, both of those words translate to "proverb," there is, in fact, a distinction between these two concepts. **А пословица** (poslovitsa) typically has a moral contained therein, while a **pogovorka** (поговорка) is more of a common saying. These vary by region.

have you heard of an Irish goodbye where you leave a party without saying goodbye? Well a Jewish goodbye is the exact opposite -**прощаемся и не уходим** [proshaemsa y ne uhodim] we say goodbye but never leave..which I guess is why I keep saying I'll start the book and delaying starting

всё перемелица, мука будет- everything will be ground together and you will have flour. This expression is used to say that no matter the conflicts that happen it will be ok because we are family and we love each other. A similar American saying is "everything comes out in the wash."

Водка без пива деньги на ветер [vodka bez piva dengi na veter] Vodka without beer is money wasted. Basically to get your bang for the buck, drink both together.

my mom and dad always turn on the lights and shout out **сделай праздник** "make it a holiday" when we sit down for a meal together.

"я не могу прийти с пустыми руками" I cannot go somewhere with my hands empty, or I can't got so someone's house without bringing something

Кончил дело гуляй смело, if you're finished with tasks then party freely or work first party second.

Из гавна конфетку- literally to make candy out of shit, when you have subpar ingredients and yet you can still turn them into something delicious (technically speaking the word for shit in Russian is **дерьмо** [der'mp] and this is a hybrid Ukrainian Russian phrase as some in my family inevitably are

Была бы курочка сварит и дурочка- if there was a chicken any idiot could cook it

Евреи не жалейте мяса в котлеты- Jews, don't spare meat for the cutlets, if you want something to taste good you have to use the correct ingredients (or any amount of the actual ingredient needed)

Не имéй сто рублéй, а имéй сто друзéй, It is better to have a hundred friends than a hundred rubles

Аппетит приходит во время еды | Appetite comes with eating. when you see a table laden with goodies you will get an appetite even if you didn't have one before (works for everything in life, the idea is just get started on whatever you're starting on...like reading this book for instance)

отдать всё до последней рубахи [otdai vse to posledniy rubahi] give everything away until the last shirt! We'll get to the paradox of not having any food but being able to serve your guests food in a bit.

сначала накорми потом расспроси [snachala nakormi potom rasprosi] feed someone first, ask questions later.

Коль пошла такая пьянка режь последний огурец [kol poshla takaya pyanka, rezh posledniy ogorez] if the party is still going then serve everything until the last pickle.

Давать на лапу, to give onto the paw, to bribe someone

Без труда не вытянешь рыбку из пруда | without work you will not pull the fish out of the hole lif you don't work hard you won't accomplish anything

Hot appetizers in Russian are called **промежутки** 'promezhutki', or in translation they are things that are in between. They function as transitions between things at events. For example at a wedding if guests have been dancing a while and you'd like to call people back to the table to resume the wedding program you serve a hot appetizer.

Горяче? Студи, дураче. [Gorachye? Studi durachye] Too hot? Blow on it you dummy. This is another example of a Ukrainian Russian hybrid.

the word for entree in Russian is **горячее** [gorachaye] or hot, as presumably your entrees are always served hot

хлеб драгоценность, им не сори [hleb dragozenost, im ne soree] bread is precious, do not waste it

Маленькие детки маленькие бедки подрастают детки подрастают бедки [Malen'kiye detki malen'kiye bedki podrastayut detki podrastayut bedki] The literal translation is small kids = small problems, and bigger kids = bigger problems.

возми печенье с полки [vozmi pechnye s polki] or take a cookie off the shelf to reward yourself.

this saying in Russian is **не сыпь мне соль на рану** [ne syp' mne sol' na ranu]

Всяк кули́к своё боло́то хва́лит. Every sandpiper praises his own swamp. Every cook praises their own broth.

AUTHOR BIO

Yuliya Patsay is a Soviet-born, San Francisco-raised, teller of stories - most of which are at least half true.

She loves rolling fog, dim sum and a captive receptive audience. She lives in the culinarily diverse neighborhood of 'Little Russia' with her husband, two kids, and enough mishpuha close by to keep her wildly entertained!

This is her first book, though hopefully not her last. You can find her at yuliyapatsay.com or anywhere she can grab hold of an unattended microphone.

Book Blurbs

"This book is good. You should buy it."
—Me

(But as they say Всяк кули́к своё боло́то хва́лит.
Every sandpiper praises his own swamp. Every cook praises their own broth.)

"Who's going to buy this book anyway?"
—My mother

"Very funny! This is definitely something I might turn on while I'm in the shower..."
—My best friend's husband

"This book is impossible to describe. You simply have to experience it for yourself. And you must. You simply must. Trust me. You'll thank me later."
—Mila Kunis*
*what Mila Kunis might say if she read this

"Look, I didn't have a choice. I had to read this book. But you have a choice. So make the right one."
—My oldest childhood friend, Vika